Quilt Note

What to do with all of those scraps of fabric left over from larger quilts? Why not make coasters? This book features 83 quick-to-quilt coaster patterns to give as gifts to family and friends or to keep for yourself. Whether you enjoy appliqué, strip piecing or paper piecing best, you'll find something you'll want to make from this fun collection.

General Instructions

Scraps of leftover fabrics from other projects are perfect choices to use when making coasters. If you prefer to purchase fabrics for a planned color scheme, a fat quarter (piece of fabric cut 18" x 22") of each of the fabric colors suggested with each set is usually enough to make a set. Fabrics may be prewashed before using, but it is not necessary. Fabrics should be colorfast, as coasters do get wet and require frequent washings.

Lightweight batting works best for coasters. If the coaster is too thick, a glass might be easily tipped over.

Use all-purpose sewing thread for all piecing. It may also be used for machine quilting.

Refer to the grainlines marked on each template for placing templates on fabric. The arrow indicates that the pattern piece should be placed with the arrow on the straight of grain of the fabric. The straight of grain runs parallel to the selvage or finished edged of the fabric. In Figure 1, the longest side of piece G is on the outside edge of the block and the straight of grain should be on this edge.

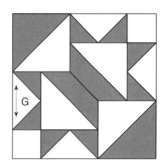

Figure 1

Appliqué Blocks

Specific instructions are given with each appliqué design to complete blocks. Appliqué templates do not include a seam allowance. If you prefer to hand-appliqué pieces, add a seam allowance when cutting pieces from fabric.

The basic method includes tracing template pieces on the paper side of fusible web, leaving a space between each piece. Trace the number of each piece as indicated on pattern pieces or in cutting charts. Cut out shapes, leaving a margin around each shape. Fuse shapes to the wrong side of the fabrics as indicated on pattern pieces or cutting charts for color. Cut out shapes on traced lines; remove paper backing.

Place pieces on background, layering in numerical order as marked on the diagram; fuse in place referring to manufacturer's instructions.

Using a narrow zigzag stitch and thread suggested in the instructions or list of materials, machine-appliqué pieces in place.

Pieced Blocks

The templates needed are listed in the instructions for each design. A ¼" seam allowance has been added to each template used in pieced blocks to make machine-piecing easy. Some templates are used for more than one design. These templates are found on pages 63 and 64.

Piece each block in units, referring to the piecing diagrams given with each pattern. Join the units to complete the block; press when complete.

Paper-Pieced Blocks

Copy or trace the full-size paper-piecing patterns for each coaster. *Note: Fabric pieces will be placed on the front of the pattern; sewing will be done on the back of the pattern. If pattern lines are not visible on the back, trace lines on the back also.*

Cut a scrap of fabric at least ¼" larger on all sides than each area. Place fabric over area 1 on pattern front. Place area 2 fabric right sides together over area 1 fabric. Set machine for 14–18 stitches per inch. Stitch on pattern back along the line between areas 1 and 2 beginning one stitch before line and ending one stitch beyond line. Trim seam allowance. Fold fabric 2 over area 2 on the pattern; press seam open.

Continue to add pieces following the numerical order and fabric colors on pattern to complete each block section. *Note: Some blocks are pieced in sections. Sew block sections together to form completed block.* Trim to the outside of block seam allowance. Leave paper pattern intact.

Cut backing and batting pieces as indicated for each coaster set. Place pieced coaster top right sides together with a backing piece; place a batting piece under backing piece as shown in Figure 2. Sew around edge along sewing line; leave a 2" opening on one side.

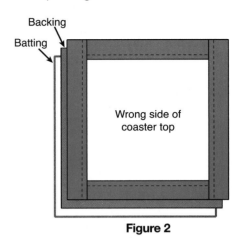

Figure 2

Remove paper pattern. Turn right side out. Hand-stitch opening closed. Hand- or machine-quilt as desired.

Binding

The coasters may be finished in a number of methods. One method is to lay the finished block right sides together with the backing. Place batting piece on top. Sew a ¼" seam all around outside edges, leaving a 2" opening on one side. Trim corners; turn right side out through opening and press. Hand-stitch opening closed to finish.

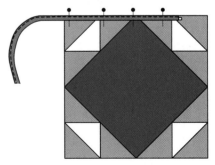

Figure 3

Piping may be added to the edges before sewing the layers together. Measure distance around coaster edges; cut a piece of piping this length plus 3". Pin to pieced block as shown in Figure 3. Sew all around, overlapping at the beginning and end; trim excess. Finish coaster using method given for unbound edges in previous paragraph to complete.

A second method is to bind the edges with either self-made or purchased binding. The instructions for coasters include 2¾ yards self-made or purchased binding in the list of materials. Most of the coasters use four 1½" x 5½" fabric strips of coordinating fabric which may be cut on the bias or on the straight of grain.

To bind edges, fold in ½" on one long edge of each strip; press. Place one strip with remaining raw edge right sides together with the top side of the coaster; stitch. Trim ends even with coaster as shown in Figure 4. Fold strip to the back side; hand-stitch in place. Repeat with a second strip on the adjacent side, turning one end in ¼" as shown in Figure 5. Continue adding strips, centering the final strip. Turn both ends of final strip under ¼", again referring to Figure 5. Fold strip to back side and hand-stitch in place to finish.

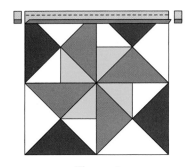

Figure 4

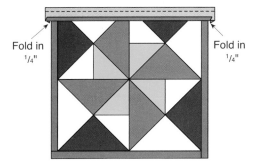

Fold in ¼"   Fold in ¼"

Figure 5

If you prefer to use one long strip for binding, prepare a 1½" x 96" strip of coordinating fabric; press under ¼" on one long edge. Stitch to

coaster, starting on one side. Continue stitching around each side, either mitering or rounding corners as shown in Figure 6. When you have reached the starting point, overlap beginning point as shown in Figure 7, folding raw end under ⅛", and stitch. Turn binding to back side; hand-stitch in place.

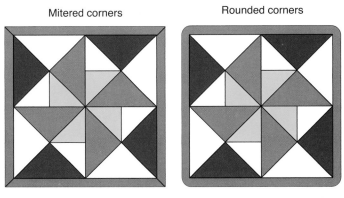

Mitered corners   Rounded corners

Figure 6

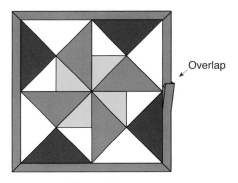

Overlap

Figure 7

Quilting

You may choose to hand- or machine-quilt your finished coasters. The samples shown were machine-quilted in the ditch of some seams to hold the layers together. Because these are small projects and probably won't be family heirlooms, machine quilting is the preferred method. All-purpose or machine-quilting thread to match background fabrics or clear nylon monofilament may be used. If using monofilament in the top of the machine, use all-purpose thread to match backing in the bobbin. ■

Spring Is Here

BY RUTH M. SWASEY

Pale pastel fabrics remind us of spring and the first days of warm weather.

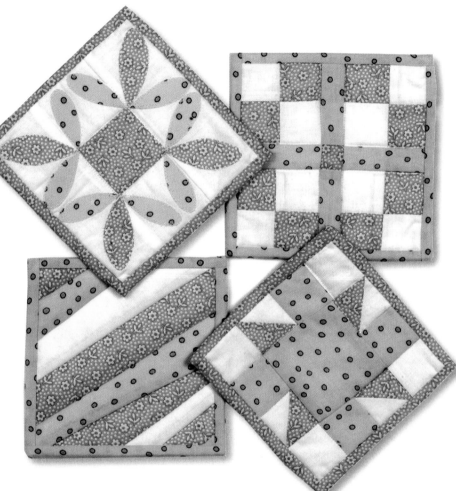

PROJECT SPECIFICATIONS
Coaster Size: 5" x 5"
Block Size: 4½" x 4½"
Number of Blocks: 4

MATERIALS FOR THE SET
- Fat quarter each pink and green prints
- Fat quarter white solid
- 12" x 12" square backing fabric
- 12" x 12" square light-weight batting
- 2¾ yards self-made or purchased binding
- White all-purpose thread
- ⅛ yard fusible web
- Basic sewing tools and supplies

INSTRUCTIONS
1. Cut four squares batting 5" x 5" and four squares backing fabric 5" x 5". Cut four 24" pieces prepared bias binding.

2. Prepare templates using pattern pieces given. Cut as directed for each coaster as indicated in separate cutting charts.

3. Join pieces to make units referring to unit piecing diagram given for each design. Join units to complete blocks referring to the block piecing diagram given for each block.

4. Finish coasters referring to Binding and Quilting instructions on pages 2 and 3.

Honeybee Instructions
1. For Honeybee design, trace pieces 1 and 2 onto paper side of fusible web referring to the cutting chart for number to cut. Cut out shapes leaving a margin around each piece. Fuse shapes to the wrong side of fabrics referring to the cutting chart for color. Cut out shapes on traced lines; remove paper backing.

2. Arrange and fuse shapes on pieced block referring to Figure 1 and following manufacturer's instructions.

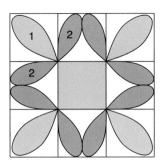

Figure 1

Stripped Pastel

1. Place one batting square on the wrong side of one backing square; pin layers together.

2. Cut random strips from pink and green prints and white solid to fit across diagonal of square.

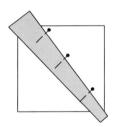

Figure 2

Figure 3

3. Pin one strip in the center as shown in Figure 2; pin a second strip right sides together with the first strip; stitch through all layers as shown in Figure 3. Press strips open.

4. Pin another strip on each of the stitched strips; stitch and press. Continue adding strips until square is covered.

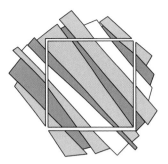

Figure 4

5. Trim excess fabric from strips even with backing square as shown in Figure 4 to finish piecing. ■

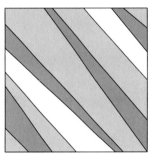

Stripped Pastel
Placement Diagram
5" x 5"

**Honeybee Template
Cutting Chart**

1—Cut 4 pink print

2—Cut 8 green print

L—Cut 1 pink print
& 8 white solid

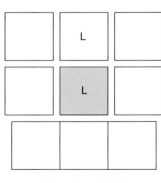

Honeybee Units
Piece units as shown.

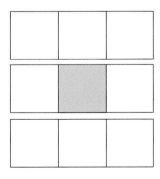

Honeybee
Block Piecing Diagram
Lay out pieces to complete 1
Honeybee block.

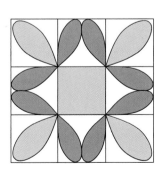

Honeybee
Placement Diagram
5" x 5"

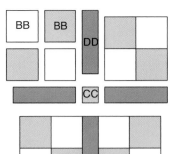

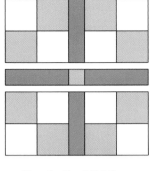

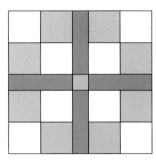

Man in the Middle Template Cutting Chart

BB—Cut 8 each pink print & white solid

CC—Cut 1 pink print

DD—Cut 4 green print

Man in the Middle Units
Piece units as shown.

Man in the Middle
Block Piecing Diagram
Lay out pieces to complete 1
Man in the Middle block.

Man in the Middle
Placement Diagram
5" x 5"

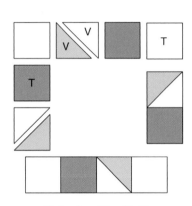

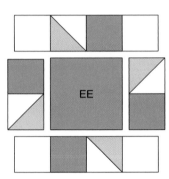

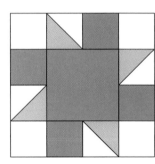

Spinning Star Template Cutting Chart

EE—Cut 1 green print

T—Cut 4 each white solid & green print

V—Cut 4 each pink print & white solid

Spinning Star Units
Piece units as shown.

Spinning Star
Block Piecing Diagram
Lay out pieces to complete 1
Spinning Star block.

Spinning Star
Placement Diagram
5" x 5"

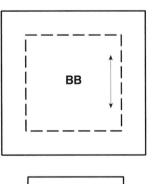

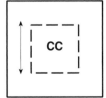

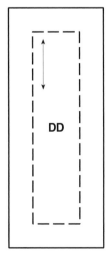

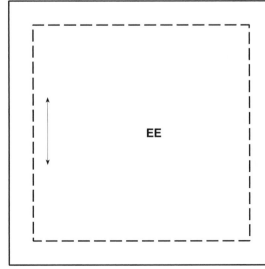

Summer Blooms

BY SUE HARVEY

Flower shapes detailed with quilting lines make quick and easy coasters.

PROJECT SPECIFICATIONS
Coaster Size: Approximately 4½" x 5"
Block Size: Approximately 4½" x 5"
Number of Blocks: 4

MATERIALS FOR THE SET
- 12" x 12" square each light pink, burgundy, yellow and lavender mottled solids
- 12" x 12" square batting
- All-purpose thread to match each fabric
- Basic sewing supplies and tools

INSTRUCTIONS

1. Trace the cutting and sewing lines for each flower on the back of the appropriate fabrics.

2. For each flower, place same-color pieces right sides together; place batting under and pin. Cut along outside line.

3. Place flower front onto the pattern, right side up; trace the dashed quilting lines onto the flower front, using a light box or, if necessary, taping both to a window to see lines.

4. Place flower back onto the pattern, right side up; trace the dashed sewing line onto the flower back.

5. Place flower front and back right sides together with batting under the flower front; pin.

6. Stitch along the sewing line marked on the flower back fabric, leaving a 2" opening on one side. Turn right sides out through opening. Hand-stitch the opening closed with matching thread.

7. Hand- or machine-quilt along the marked quilting lines to finish. ∎

Pansy Coaster
Placement Diagram
Approximately 4¹⁄₂" x 5"

Peony Coaster
Placement Diagram
Approximately 4¹⁄₂" x 5"

Rose Coaster
Placement Diagram
Approximately 4¹⁄₂" x 5"

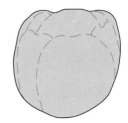

Tulip Coaster
Placement Diagram
Approximately 4¹⁄₂" x 5"

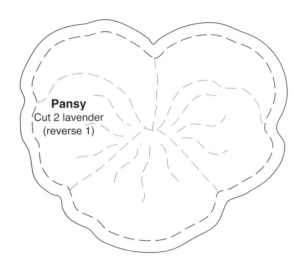

Pansy
Cut 2 lavender
(reverse 1)

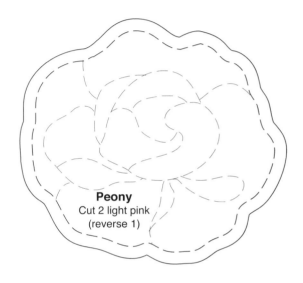

Peony
Cut 2 light pink
(reverse 1)

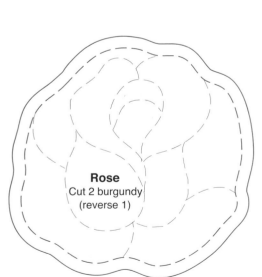

Rose
Cut 2 burgundy
(reverse 1)

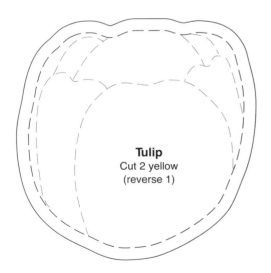

Tulip
Cut 2 yellow
(reverse 1)

Going in Circles

BY RUTH M. SWASEY

This coaster set includes curved pieces and some simple machine appliqué for a fun set.

PROJECT SPECIFICATIONS
Coaster Size: 5" diameter
Block Size: 4½" diameter
Number of Blocks: 4

MATERIALS FOR THE SET
- Fat quarter each pink, blue and white prints
- 12" x 12" square backing fabric
- 12" x 12" square lightweight batting
- 2 yards self-made or purchased binding
- White all-purpose thread
- 8" x 8" square fusible web
- Basic sewing tools and supplies

Instructions
1. Cut four squares batting 5" x 5" and four squares backing fabric 5" x 5". Cut four 18" pieces prepared bias binding.

2. Prepare templates using pattern pieces given. Cut as directed for each coaster as indicated in separate cutting charts.

3. Join pieces to make units referring to unit piecing diagram given for each design. Join units to complete blocks referring to the block piecing diagram given for each block.

4. Using the pieced blocks as a pattern, trim backing and batting even with blocks.

5. Finish coasters referring to Binding and Quilting instructions on pages 2 and 3.

Meet in the Middle
1. Cut a 5" circle blue print using the QQ template on page 63.

2. Trace four RR pieces on the paper side of the fusible web, leaving space between each piece. Cut out shapes leaving a margin around each piece. Fuse to the wrong side of pink print. Cut out RR pieces on traced lines; remove paper backing.

3. Arrange RR shapes on the QQ circle with points touching in the center; fuse in place referring to manufacturer's instructions.

4. Use a narrow zigzag stitch to secure pieces in place to finish block.

Wheel

1. Trace the TT circle on the paper side of the remaining fusible web. Fuse to the wrong side of blue print. Cut out TT on traced line; remove paper backing.

2. Join SS pieces referring to the piecing diagram.

3. Sandwich a batting piece between a backing piece and the pieced SS unit; pin layers together.

4. Fuse the TT circle over the center of the pieced SS unit. Use a narrow zigzag stitch to secure pieces in place to finish block. ■

Circle Star Template Cutting Chart

OO—Cut 8 blue print

PP—Cut 4 each white & pink prints

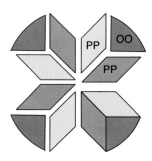

Circle Star Units
Piece units as shown.

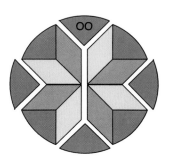

Circle Star
Block Piecing Diagram
Lay out pieces to complete
1 Circle Star block.

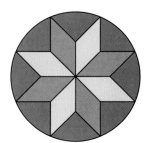

Circle Star
Placement Diagram
5" diameter

Meet in the Middle Template Cutting Chart

QQ—Cut 1 blue print

RR—Cut 4 pink print

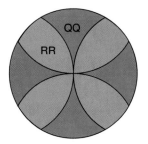

Meet in the Middle Units
Arrange RR pieces on QQ as shown.

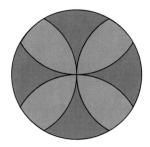

Meet in the Middle
Placement Diagram
5" diameter

Swirling Star Template Cutting Chart

LL—Cut 4 blue print

G—Cut 4 pink print

NN—Cut 1 white print

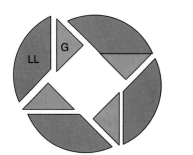

Swirling Star Units
Piece units as shown.

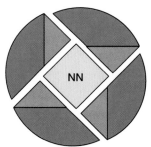

Swirling Star
Block Piecing Diagram
Lay out pieces to complete 1
Swirling Star block.

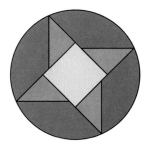

Swirling Star
Placement Diagram
5" diameter

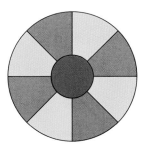

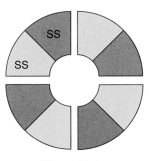

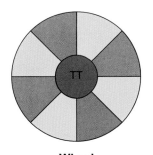

Wheel Template Cutting Chart

SS—Cut 4 each white & pink prints

TT—Cut 1 blue print

Wheel Units
Piece units as shown.

Wheel
Block Piecing Diagram
Fuse TT circle to center
of pieced unit to
complete 1 Wheel block.

Wheel
Placement Diagram
5" diameter

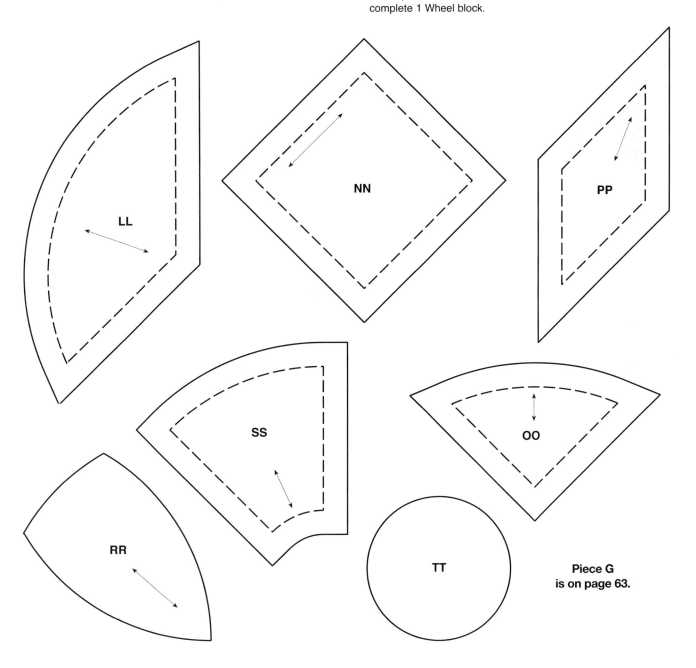

LL

NN

PP

SS

RR

OO

TT

**Piece G
is on page 63.**

1950s Coasters

BY RUTH M. SWASEY

The fabrics used to make this coaster set are reproduction fabrics from the 1950s.

PROJECT SPECIFICATIONS

Coaster Size: 5" x 5"
Block Size: 4½" x 4½"
Number of Blocks: 4

MATERIALS FOR THE SET

- Fat quarter each purple, blue and white prints
- 12" x 12" square backing fabric
- 12" x 12" square light-weight batting
- 2¾ yards self-made or purchased binding
- White all-purpose thread
- Basic sewing tools and supplies

INSTRUCTIONS

1. Cut four squares batting 5" x 5" and four squares backing fabric 5" x 5". Cut four 24" pieces prepared bias binding.

2. Prepare templates using pattern pieces given. Cut as directed for each coaster as indicated in separate cutting charts.

3. Join pieces to make units referring to unit piecing diagram given for each design. Join units to complete blocks referring to the block piecing diagram given for each block.

4. Finish coasters referring to the Binding and Quilting instructions on pages 2 and 3. ■

HOUSE OF WHITE BIRCHES, BERNE, INDIANA 46711   WWW.WHITEBIRCHES.COM

Fluttering Wings
Template Cutting Chart

HH—Cut 4 each blue &
  white prints (reverse
  half of each for HHR)

II—Cut 4 purple print

KK—Cut 2 each blue &
  white prints

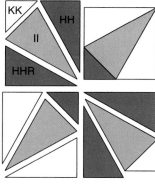

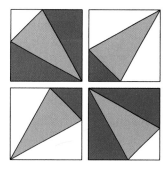

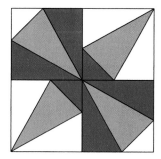

Fluttering Wings Units
Piece units as shown.

Fluttering Wings
Block Piecing Diagram
Lay out pieces to complete 1
Fluttering Wings block.

Fluttering Wings
Placement Diagram
5" x 5"

Square Surrounded
Template Cutting Chart

V—Cut 4 white print &
  12 purple print

CCC—Cut 1 blue print

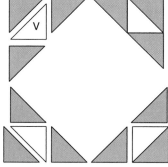

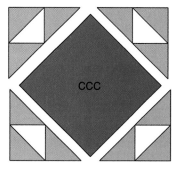

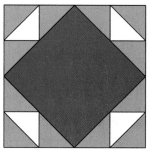

Square Surrounded Units
Piece units as shown.

Square Surrounded
Block Piecing Diagram
Lay out pieces to complete 1
Square Surrounded block.

Square Surrounded
Placement Diagram
5" x 5"

Swirling Blades
Template Cutting Chart

CCC—Cut 1 purple print

U—Cut 4 each blue &
  white prints

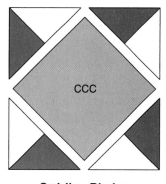

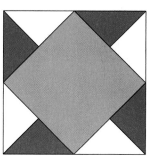

Swirling Blades Units
Piece units as shown.

Swirling Blades
Block Piecing Diagram
Lay out pieces to complete 1
Swirling Blades block.

Swirling Blades
Placement Diagram
5" x 5"

Tudor Triangles
Template Cutting Chart

GG—Cut 4 blue print

FF—Cut 4 purple print

G—Cut 4 white print

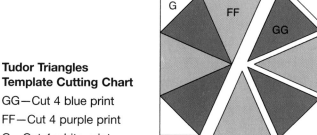

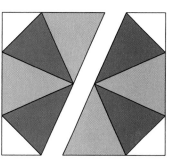

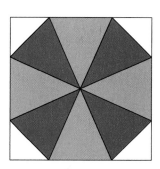

Tudor Triangles Units
Piece units as shown.

Tudor Triangles
Block Piecing Diagram
Lay out pieces to complete 1
Tudor Triangles block.

Tudor Triangles
Placement Diagram
5" x 5"

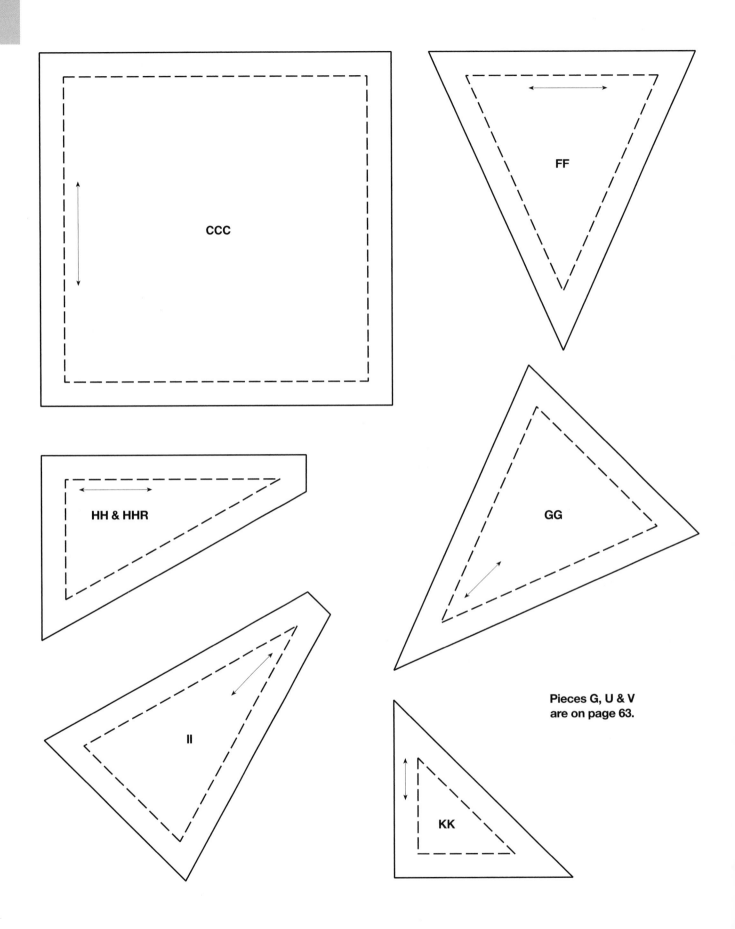

CCC

FF

HH & HHR

GG

II

Pieces G, U & V
are on page 63.

KK

Hexagon Flowers

BY RUTH M. SWASEY

Hexagon blocks are easy to stitch and add a nice variety to your coaster collection.

PROJECT SPECIFICATIONS
Coaster Size: 5¼" x 6¼"
Block Size: 4¾" x 5½"
Number of Blocks: 4

MATERIALS FOR THE SET
- Fat quarter each green and floral prints
- 16" x 16" square backing fabric
- 16" x 16" square lightweight batting
- 2¾ yards self-made or purchased binding
- Green all-purpose thread
- Basic sewing tools and supplies

INSTRUCTIONS
1. Cut four squares batting 7" x 7" and four squares backing fabric 7" x 7". Cut four 24" pieces prepared bias binding.

2. Prepare templates using pattern pieces given. Cut as directed for each coaster as indicated in separate cutting charts.

3. Join pieces to make units referring to unit piecing diagram given for each design. Join units to complete blocks referring to the block piecing diagram given for each block.

4. Trim backing and batting even with pieced coaster tops.

5. Finish coasters referring to Binding and Quilting instructions on pages 2 and 3. ■

Hexagon Maze Template Cutting Chart

UU—Cut 3 each green & floral prints

VV—Cut 3 each green & floral prints

WW—Cut 1 green print

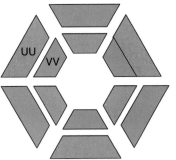

Hexagon Maze Units
Piece units as shown.

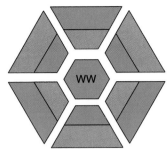

Hexagon Maze
Block Piecing Diagram
Lay out pieces to complete 1 Hexagon Maze block.

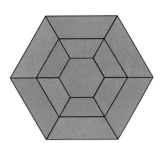
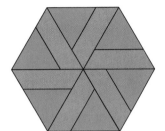

Hexagon Maze
Placement Diagram
5¼" x 6¼"

Hexagon Path Template Cutting Chart

ZZ—Cut 6 green print

YY—Cut 6 floral print

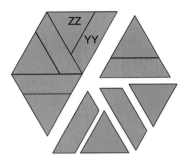

Hexagon Path Units
Piece units as shown.

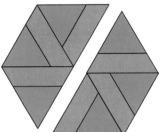

Hexagon Path
Block Piecing Diagram
Lay out pieces to complete 1 Hexagon Path block.

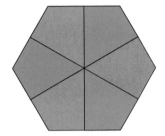

Hexagon Path
Placement Diagram
5¼" x 6¼"

Hexagon Pinwheel Template Cutting Chart

XX—Cut 3 each green & floral prints

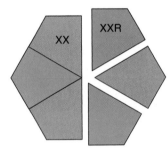
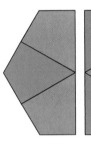

Hexagon Pinwheel Units
Piece units as shown.

Hexagon Pinwheel
Block Piecing Diagram
Lay out pieces to complete 1 Hexagon Pinwheel block.

Hexagon Pinwheel
Placement Diagram
5¼" x 6¼"

Hexagon Star Template Cutting Chart

AAA—Cut 6 green print

BBB—Cut 6 floral print

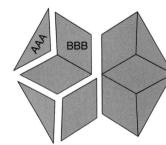

Hexagon Star Units
Piece units as shown.

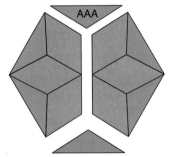

Hexagon Star
Block Piecing Diagram
Lay out pieces to complete 1 Hexagon Star block.

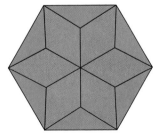

Hexagon Star
Placement Diagram
5¼" x 6¼"

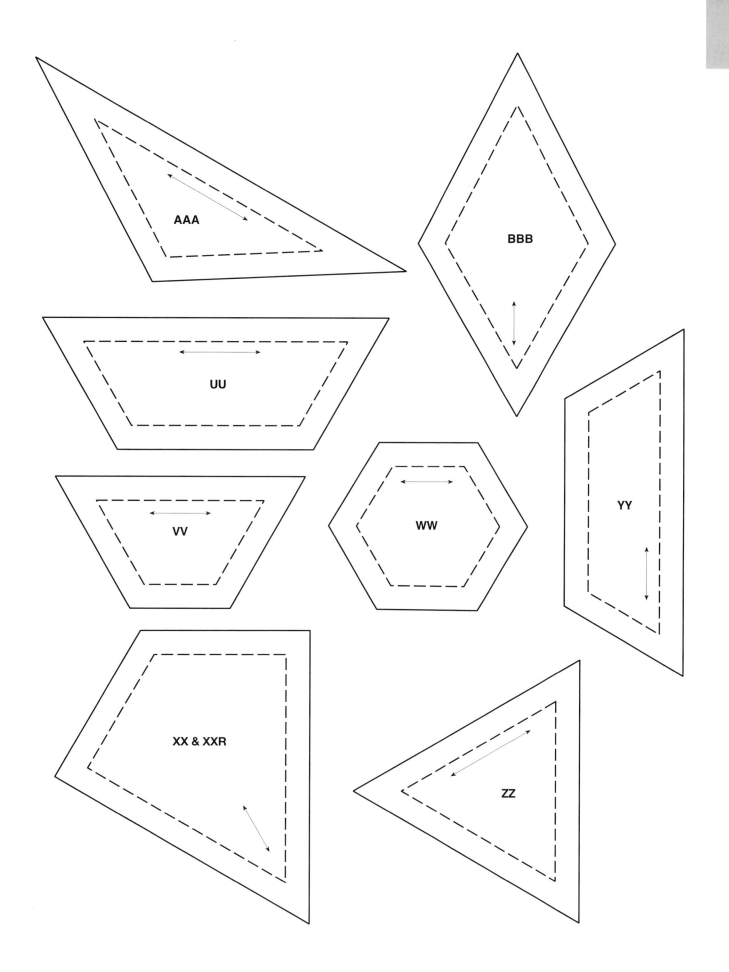

Star Shine

BY SUE HARVEY

Four different star designs are used to create this bright yellow, blue and white coaster set.

PROJECT SPECIFICATIONS

Coaster Size: 4½" x 4½"
Block Size: 4" x 4"
Number of Blocks: 4

MATERIALS FOR THE SET

- Fat quarter blue print
- 10" x 10" square each yellow and white/black prints
- 10" x 10" square batting
- Blue all-purpose thread
- Basic sewing supplies and tools

CUTTING FOR THE SET

1. Cut four squares batting 5" x 5" and four squares blue print 5" x 5" for backing.

2. Cut eight strips each blue print ¾" x 4½" and ¾" x 5" for borders.

INSTRUCTIONS

1. Prepare templates using pattern pieces given. Cut pieces as indicated for each coaster. Cut border strips, backing and batting pieces as indicated for each coaster set.

2. Follow block piecing diagrams for each pieced coaster.

3. Sew ¾" x 4½" border strips to two opposite sides of pieced coaster; press. Sew ¾" x 5" border strips to the two remaining sides to form the coaster top; press.

4. Place coaster top right sides together with backing fabric; place a batting square under backing fabric.

5. Sew around edge using a ¼" seam allowance; leave a 2" opening on one side. Turn right side out; hand-stitch opening closed.

6. Hand- or machine-quilt as desired. ∎

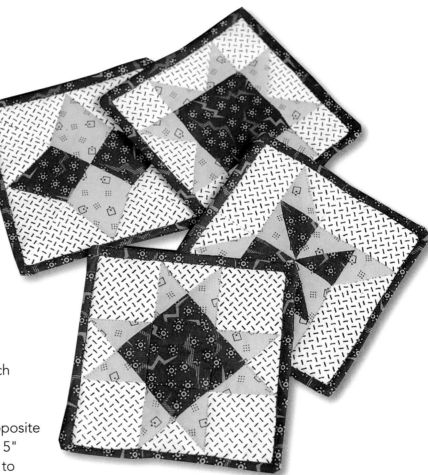

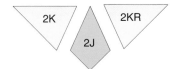

Connecting Star Units
Make 4 units.

Connecting Star Template Cutting Chart

2J—Cut 2 yellow print & 2 blue print

2K—Cut 8 white/black print; (reverse half for KR)

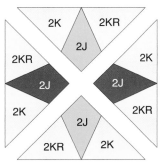

Connecting Star
Block Piecing Diagram
Lay out pieces to complete
1 Connecting Star block.

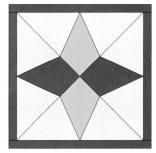

Connecting Star
Placement Diagram
4½" x 4½"

Ohio Star Units
Combine triangles as above to form
4 squares for Ohio Star block.

Ohio Star Template Cutting Chart

2L—Cut 8 yellow print & 4 each
white/black & blue prints

2C—Cut 4 white/black print &
1 blue print

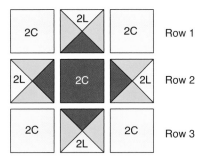

Row 1

Row 2

Row 3

Ohio Star
Block Piecing Diagram
Lay out pieces to complete 1 Ohio Star block.

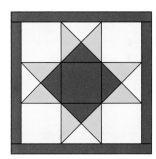

Ohio Star
Placement Diagram
4½" x 4½"

Sawtooth Star Units
Make 4 units.

Sawtooth Star Template Cutting Chart

2A—Cut 8 yellow print

2D—Cut 4 white/black print

2G—Cut 4 white/black print

2H—Cut 1 blue print

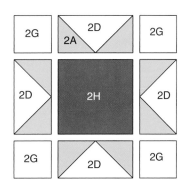

Sawtooth Star
Block Piecing Diagram
Lay out pieces to complete 1 Sawtooth
Star block.

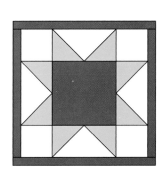

Sawtooth Star
Placement Diagram
4½" x 4½"

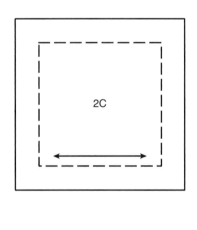

Spinning Star Units
Make 4 of each unit. Press seams toward yellow A in the yellow/white units; press seams toward the blue A in the yellow/blue units.

Spinning Star Template Cutting Chart
2A—Cut 8 yellow print & 4 each white/black & blue prints

2I—Cut 4 white/black print

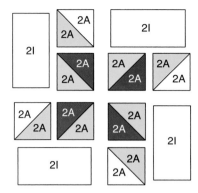

Spinning Star
Block Piecing Diagram
Lay out pieces to complete 1 Spinning Star block.

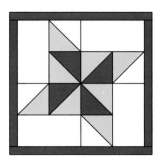

Spinning Star
Placement Diagram
4½" x 4½"

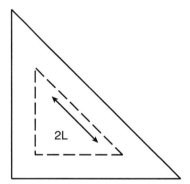

2C

2L

Remaining pattern pieces are on page 64.

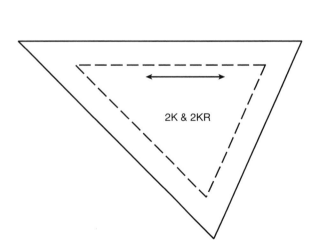

2K & 2KR

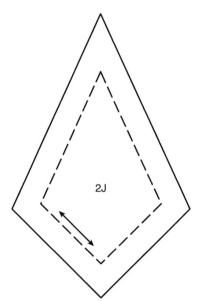

2J

Sunflower Sunshine

BY RUTH M. SWASEY

A pretty sunflower print was used as the yellow print in these coasters with a summery feel.

PROJECT SPECIFICATIONS

Coaster Size: 5" x 5"
Block Size: 4½" x 4½"
Number of Blocks: 4

MATERIALS FOR THE SET

- Fat quarter each white, blue and yellow prints
- 12" x 12" square backing fabric
- 12" x 12" square lightweight batting
- 2¾ yards self-made or purchased binding
- White all-purpose thread
- Basic sewing tools and supplies

INSTRUCTIONS

1. Cut four squares batting 5" x 5" and four squares backing fabric 5" x 5". Cut four 24" pieces prepared bias binding.

2. Prepare templates using pattern pieces given. Cut as directed for each coaster as indicated in separate cutting charts.

3. Join pieces to make units referring to the unit piecing diagram given for each design. Join units to complete blocks referring to the block piecing diagram given for each block.

4. Finish coasters referring to Binding and Quilting instructions on pages 2 and 3. ■

Sunflower Blossom Template Cutting Chart

P—Cut 1 blue print

T—Cut 1 each blue & white prints

U—Cut 2 white print

W—Cut 1 white print

X—Cut 4 yellow print (reverse half for XR)

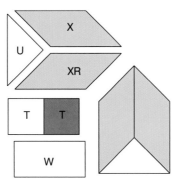

Sunflower Blossom Units
Piece units as shown.

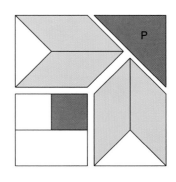

Sunflower Blossom
Block Piecing Diagram
Lay out pieces to complete 1 Sunflower Blossom block.

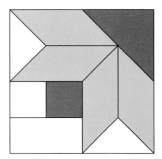

Sunflower Blossom
Placement Diagram
5" x 5"

Sunflower Cross Template Cutting Chart

I—Cut 4 each yellow & blue prints

L—Cut 1 yellow print & 4 white print

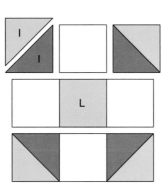

Sunflower Cross Units
Piece units as shown.

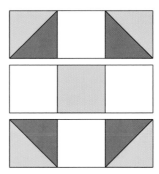

Sunflower Cross
Block Piecing Diagram
Lay out pieces to complete 1 Sunflower Cross block.

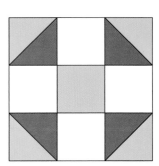

Sunflower Cross
Placement Diagram
5" x 5"

Sunflower Pinwheel Template Cutting Chart

V—Cut 4 white print & 8 blue print

Y—Cut 4 yellow print

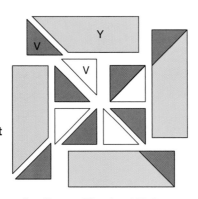

Sunflower Pinwheel Units
Piece units as shown.

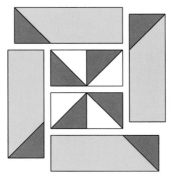

Sunflower Pinwheel
Block Piecing Diagram
Lay out pieces to complete 1 Sunflower Pinwheel block.

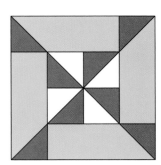

Sunflower Pinwheel
Placement Diagram
5" x 5"

Sunflower Prism Template Cutting Chart

EEE—Cut 1 blue print & 4 each yellow and white prints

F—Cut 4 each yellow & blue prints

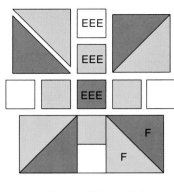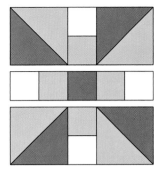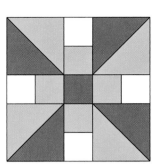

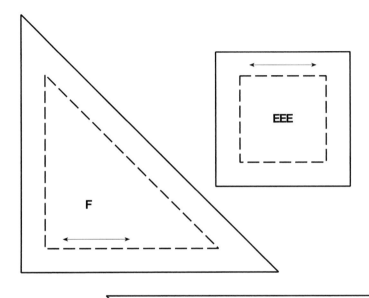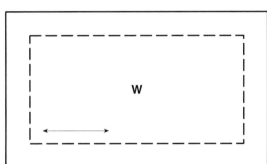

Sunflower Prism Units
Piece units as shown.

Sunflower Prism
Block Piecing Diagram
Lay out pieces to complete 1
Sunflower Prism block.

Sunflower Prism
Placement Diagram
5" x 5"

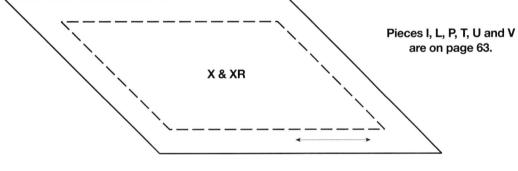

Pieces I, L, P, T, U and V
are on page 63.

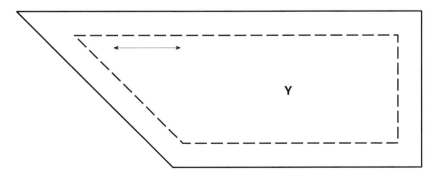

1930s Coasters
BY RUTH M. SWASEY

Reproductions of 1930s fabrics are used to make this pretty pastel coaster set.

PROJECT SPECIFICATIONS
Coaster Size: 5" x 5"
Block Size: 4½" x 4½"
Number of Blocks: 4

MATERIALS FOR THE SET
- Fat quarter each 2 red, 2 blue, yellow and white prints
- 12" x 12" square backing fabric
- 12" x 12" square lightweight batting
- 2¾ yards self-made or purchased binding
- White all-purpose thread
- Basic sewing tools and supplies

INSTRUCTIONS
1. Cut four squares batting 5" x 5" and four squares backing fabric 5" x 5". Cut four 24" pieces prepared bias binding.

2. Prepare templates using pattern pieces given. Cut as directed for each coaster as indicated in separate cutting charts.

3. Join pieces to make units referring to unit piecing diagram given for each design. Join units to complete blocks referring to the block piecing diagram given for each block.

4. Finish coasters referring to the Binding and Quilting instructions on pages 2 and 3. ∎

Stop stitching   Finish seam

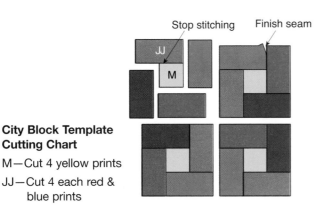

City Block Template Cutting Chart

M—Cut 4 yellow prints
JJ—Cut 4 each red & blue prints

City Block Units
Piece units as shown.

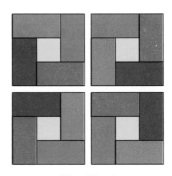

City Block
Block Piecing Diagram
Lay out pieces to complete
1 City Block block.

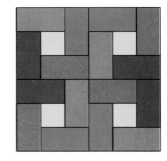

City Block
Placement Diagram
5" x 5"

Face-Off Template Cutting Chart

Q—Cut 2 each red & blue prints & 8 white print

R—Cut 1 each red & blue prints

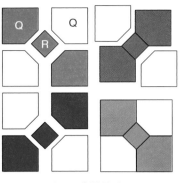

Face-Off Units
Piece units as shown.

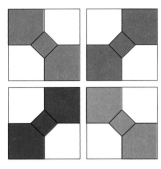

Face-Off
Block Piecing Diagram
Lay out pieces to complete 1
Face-Off block.

Face-Off
Placement Diagram
5" x 5"

Spinning Pinwheel Template Cutting Chart

U—Cut 4 each 1 red, 1 blue & white prints

V—Cut 4 each yellow & white prints

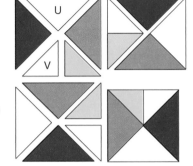

Spinning Pinwheel Units
Piece units as shown.

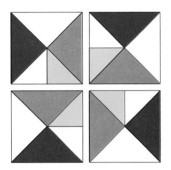

Spinning Pinwheel
Block Piecing Diagram
Lay out pieces to complete 1
Spinning Pinwheel block.

Spinning Pinwheel
Placement Diagram
5" x 5"

Spools Template Cutting Chart

S—Cut 4 each 1 red & 1 blue prints & 8 white print

T—Cut 2 each 1 red & 1 blue prints

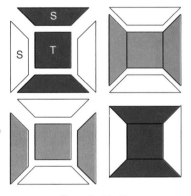

Spools Units
Piece units as shown.

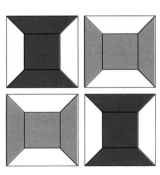

Spools
Block Piecing Diagram
Lay out pieces to complete 1
Spools block.

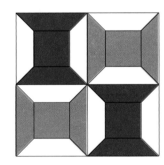

Spools
Placement Diagram
5" x 5"

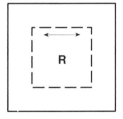

**Pieces M, T, U and V
are on page 63.**

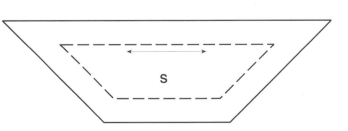

Christmas Coasters

BY RUTH M. SWASEY

The Christmas holidays are the perfect time for using these delightful coasters.

PROJECT SPECIFICATIONS

Coaster Size: 5" x 5"
Block Size: 4½" x 4½"
Number of Blocks: 4

MATERIALS FOR THE SET

- Fat quarter each green and white prints
- 12" x 12" square backing fabric
- 12" x 12" square light-weight batting
- 2¾ yards self-made or purchased binding
- White all-purpose thread
- Basic sewing tools and supplies

INSTRUCTIONS

1. Cut four squares batting 5" x 5" and four squares backing fabric 5" x 5". Cut four 24" pieces prepared bias binding.

2. Prepare templates using pattern pieces given. Cut as directed for each coaster as indicated in separate cutting charts.

3. Join pieces to make units referring to unit piecing diagram given for each design. Join units to complete blocks referring to the block piecing diagram given for each block.

4. Finish coasters referring to Binding and Quilting instructions on pages 2 and 3. ∎

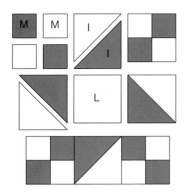

Chinese Coin Units
Piece units as shown.

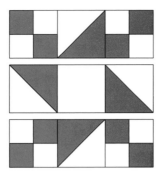

Chinese Coin
Block Piecing Diagram
Lay out pieces to complete 1
Chinese Coin block.

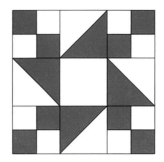

Chinese Coin
Placement Diagram
5" x 5"

Chinese Coin Template Cutting Chart

I—Cut 4 each green & white prints

L—Cut 1 white print

M—Cut 8 each white & green prints

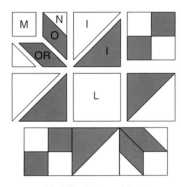

Dublin Steps Units
Piece units as shown.

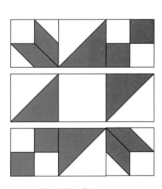

Dublin Steps
Block Piecing Diagram
Lay out pieces to complete
1 Dublin Steps block.

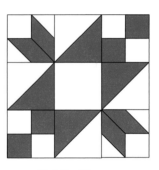

Dublin Steps
Placement Diagram
5" x 5"

Dublin Steps Template Cutting Chart

I—Cut 4 each white & green prints

L—Cut 1 white print

M—Cut 6 white print & 4 green print

N—Cut 4 white print

O—Cut 4 green print (reverse half for OR)

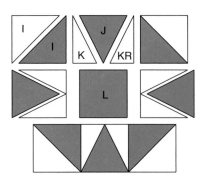

Eight-Pointed Star Units
Piece units as shown.

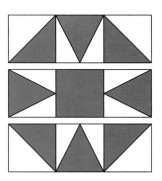

Eight-Pointed Star
Block Piecing Diagram
Lay out pieces to complete 1
Eight-Pointed Star block.

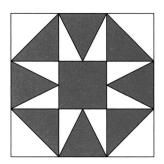

Eight-Pointed Star
Placement Diagram
5" x 5"

Eight-Pointed Star Template Cutting Chart

I—Cut 4 each white & green prints

J—Cut 4 green print

K—Cut 8 white print (reverse half for KR)

L—Cut 1 green print

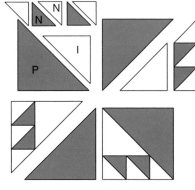

Rosebud Units
Piece units as shown.

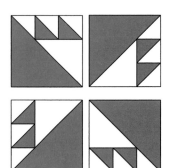

Rosebud
Block Piecing Diagram
Lay out pieces to complete
1 Rosebud block.

Rosebud
Placement Diagram
5" x 5"

Rosebud Template Cutting Chart

I—Cut 4 white print

N—Cut 8 green print & 12 white print

P—Cut 4 green print

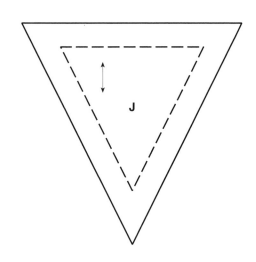

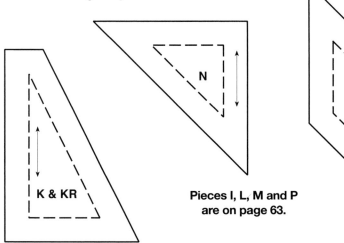

**Pieces I, L, M and P
are on page 63.**

Those Old Animals

BY SUE HARVEY

Creatures great and small have quilt block designs named for them.

PROJECT SPECIFICATIONS

Coaster Size: 4½" x 4½"
Block Size: 4" x 4"
Number of Blocks: 4

MATERIALS FOR THE SET

- Fat quarter neutral taupe plaid for background
- Scraps several plaids in assorted colors
- Scraps 6 green plaids
- Scraps 6 blue plaids
- Fat quarter black solid for backing and borders
- 10" x 10" square batting
- 1 spool each cream and black all-purpose thread
- Basic sewing supplies and tools

CUTTING FOR THE SET

1. Cut four squares each backing and batting 5" x 5".

2. Cut eight strips black solid ¾" x 4½" for borders.

3. Cut eight strips black solid ¾" x 5" for borders.

INSTRUCTIONS

1. Prepare templates using pattern pieces given. Cut pieces as indicated for each coaster. Cut border strips, backing and batting pieces as indicated for each coaster set.

2. Follow block piecing diagrams for each pieced coaster.

3. Sew ¾" x 4½" border strips to two opposite sides of pieced coaster; press. Sew ¾" x 5" border strips to the two remaining sides to form the coaster top; press.

4. Place coaster top right sides together with backing fabric; place a batting square under backing fabric.

5. Sew around edge using a ¼" seam allowance; leave a 2" opening on one side. Turn right side out; hand-stitch opening closed.

6. Hand- or machine-quilt as desired. ∎

All pattern pieces are on page 64.

Birds in the Air Template Cutting Chart

2A—Cut 6 background & 10 assorted plaids

2E—Cut 1 background

Birds in the Air Units
Join triangles to make units.

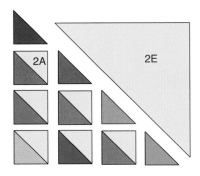

Birds in the Air
Block Piecing Diagram
Layout pieces to complete
1 Birds in the Air block.

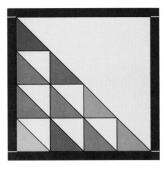

Birds in the Air
Placement Diagram
4¹/₂" x 4¹/₂"

Fox & Geese Template Cutting Chart

2A—Cut 6 assorted plaids & 10 background

2B—Cut 2 dark plaid

2G—Cut 4 background

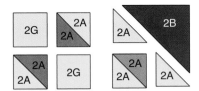

Fox & Geese Units
Piece quarters of block as shown.

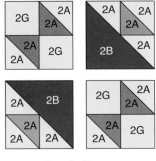

Fox & Geese
Block Piecing Diagram
Layout pieces to complete
1 Fox & Geese block.

Fox & Geese
Placement Diagram
4¹/₂" x 4¹/₂"

Snail's Trail Template Cutting Chart

2A—Cut 3 each assorted green & blue plaids & 6 background

2F—Cut 1 each green & blue plaids & 2 background

2G—Cut 2 each assorted green & blue plaids

2I—Cut 2 background

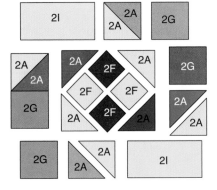

Snail's Trail Units
Piece units, placing green pieces on one side and blue on other side as shown.

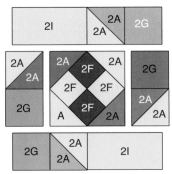

Snail's Trail
Block Piecing Diagram
Join units to complete 1 block.

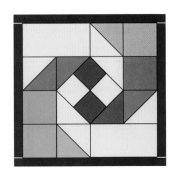

Snail's Trail
Placement Diagram
4¹/₂" x 4¹/₂"

Wild Goose Chase Template Cutting Chart

2A—Cut 16 background

2D—Cut 8 assorted plaids

Wild Goose Chase Units
Piece quarters as shown.

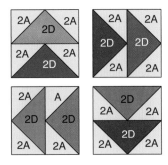

Wild Goose Chase
Block Piecing Diagram
Lay out pieces to complete 1 Wild Goose Chase block.

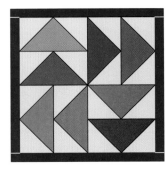

Wild Goose Chase
Placement Diagram
4¹/₂" x 4¹/₂"

Red & White Delight

BY RUTH M. SWASEY

The contrast between the red and white fabrics makes these designs stand out.

PROJECT SPECIFICATIONS
Coaster Size: 4⅞" x 4⅞"
Block Size: 4⅜" x 4⅜"
Number of Blocks: 4

MATERIALS FOR THE SET

- Fat quarter each red and white prints
- 12" x 12" square backing fabric
- 12" x 12" square light-weight batting
- 2¾ yards self-made or purchased binding
- White all-purpose thread
- Basic sewing tools and supplies

INSTRUCTIONS

1. Cut four squares batting 4⅞" x 4⅞" and four squares backing fabric 4⅞" x 4⅞". Cut four 24" pieces prepared bias binding.

2. Prepare templates using pattern pieces given. Cut as directed for each coaster as indicated in separate cutting charts.

3. Join pieces to make units referring to unit piecing diagram given for each design. Join units to complete blocks referring to the block piecing diagram given for each block.

4. Finish coasters referring to Binding and Quilting instructions on pages 2 and 3. ■

Baseball Diamond Template Cutting Chart

A—Cut 1 red print

E—Cut 1 each red & white prints

C—Cut 8 each red & white prints

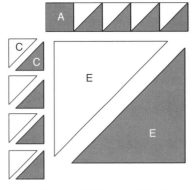

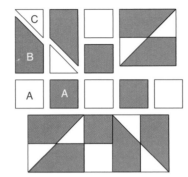

Baseball Diamond Units
Piece units as shown.

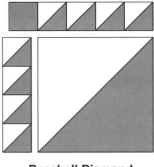

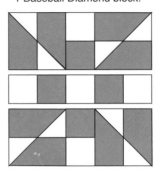

Baseball Diamond
Block Piecing Diagram
Lay out pieces to complete
1 Baseball Diamond block.

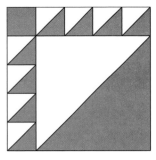

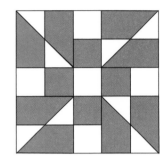

Baseball Diamond
Placement Diagram
$4^7/8$" x $4^7/8$"

Crazy Horse Template Cutting Chart

A—Cut 4 red print & 5 white print

B—Cut 8 red print

C—Cut 8 white print

Crazy Horse Units
Piece units as shown.

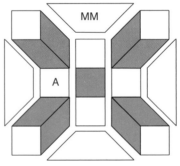

Crazy Horse
Block Piecing Diagram
Lay out pieces to complete
1 Crazy Horse block.

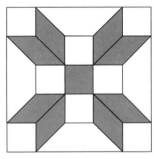

Crazy Horse
Placement Diagram
$4^7/8$" x $4^7/8$"

Farmer's Daughter Template Cutting Chart

A—Cut 1 red print & 8 white print

D—Cut 8 red print (reverse half for DR)

MM—Cut 4 white print

Farmer's Daughter Units
Piece units as shown.

Farmer's Daughter
Block Piecing Diagram
Lay out pieces to complete
1 Farmer's Daughter block.

Farmer's Daughter
Placement Diagram
4 7/8" x 4 7/8"

Queen's Crown Template Cutting Chart

A—Cut 2 white print

C—Cut 8 red print

DDD—Cut 2 red print & 4 white print

G—Cut 4 white print

H—Cut 2 red print

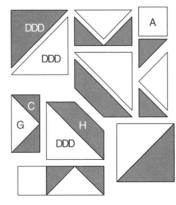

Queen's Crown Units
Piece units as shown.

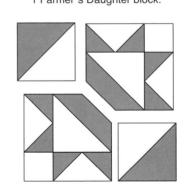

Queen's Crown
Block Piecing Diagram
Lay out pieces to complete
1 Queen's Crown block.

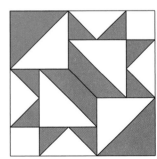

Queen's Crown
Placement Diagram
$4^7/8$" x $4^7/8$"

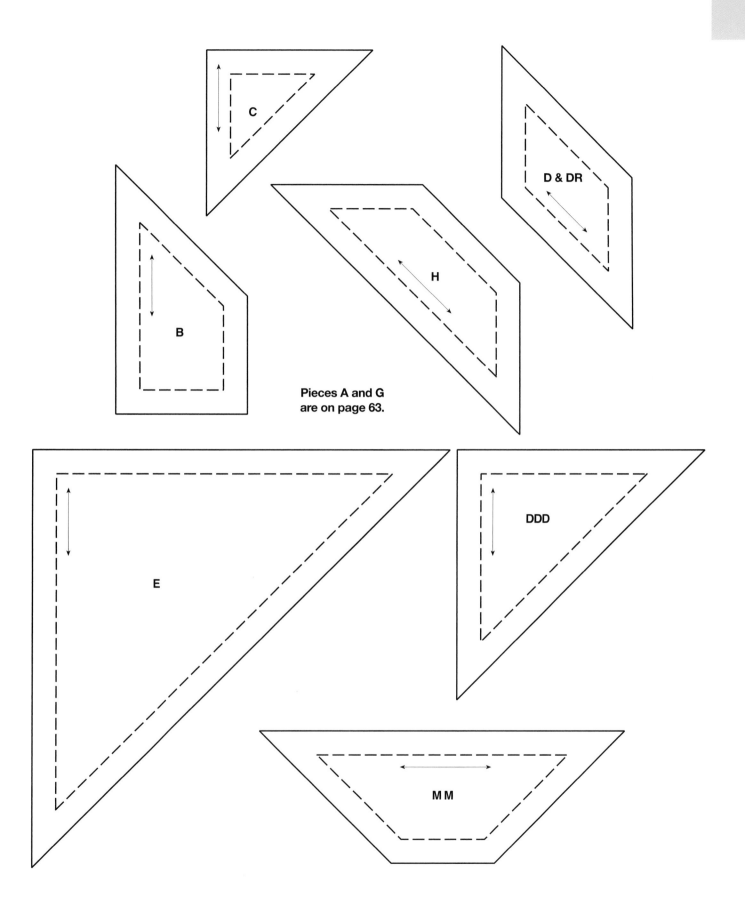

Pieces A and G
are on page 63.

Heart & Home
BY SUE HARVEY

These heart-shaped coasters are filled with houses or trees. Use bright colors or pastels to fit your decorating pleasure.

PROJECT SPECIFICATIONS
Coaster Size: 4½" x 5"
Block Size: 2½" x 2½"
Number of Blocks: 4

MATERIALS FOR THE SET
- Scraps cream, rust, black and brown solids; red, dark red, blue, brown, light green, medium green and dark green prints for house and tree blocks
- Assorted scraps for crazy-patch heart border
- 12" x 12" square black solid for backing
- 12" x 12" square batting
- Black all-purpose thread for piecing
- Basic sewing supplies and tools and tracing paper

CUTTING FOR THE SET
1. Cut four heart-shaped black solid backing pieces and four heart-shaped batting pieces using paper-pieced heart as template.

INSTRUCTIONS
1. Follow instructions for Paper-Pieced Blocks on page 2 to complete the house and tree blocks.

2. Copy or trace a full-size heart pattern for each coaster.

3. Place a paper-pieced house or tree block in center of heart-shaped paper pattern; align outer

edge of the house block with the dashed line on the heart pattern.

4. Place area 1 fabric right sides together with paper-pieced house or tree block; follow instructions for Paper-Pieced Blocks on page 2 to complete coaster.

5. Repeat for remaining house block and two tree blocks. ∎

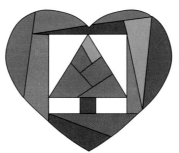

Heart/House 1 Coaster
Placement Diagram
Approximately 4½" x 5"

Heart/House 2 Coaster
Placement Diagram
Approximately 4½" x 5"

Heart/Tree 1 Coaster
Placement Diagram
Approximately 4½" x 5"

Heart/Tree 2 Coaster
Placement Diagram
Approximately 4½" x 5"

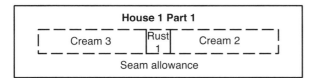

House 1 Part 1

Cream 3 | Rust 1 | Cream 2
Seam allowance

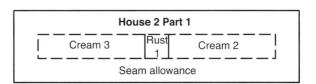

House 2 Part 1

Cream 3 | Rust 1 | Cream 2
Seam allowance

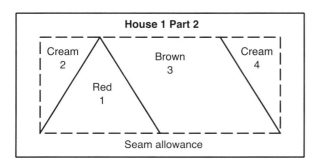

House 1 Part 2

Cream 2 | Red 1 | Brown 3 | Cream 4
Seam allowance

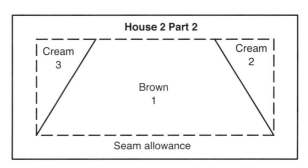

House 2 Part 2

Cream 3 | Brown 1 | Cream 2
Seam allowance

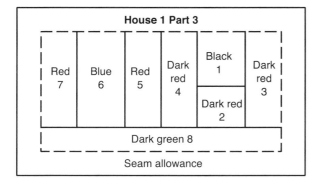

House 1 Part 3

Red 7 | Blue 6 | Red 5 | Dark red 4 | Black 1 | Dark red 3
Dark red 2
Dark green 8
Seam allowance

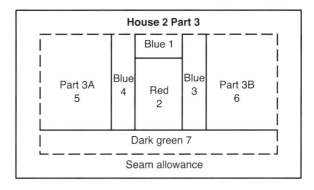

House 2 Part 3

Blue 1
Part 3A 5 | Blue 4 | Red 2 | Blue 3 | Part 3B 6
Dark green 7
Seam allowance

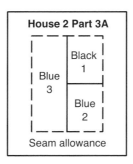

House 2 Part 3A

Blue 3 | Black 1
Blue 2
Seam allowance

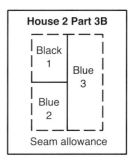

House 2 Part 3B

Black 1 | Blue 3
Blue 2
Seam allowance

Tree 1 Part 1

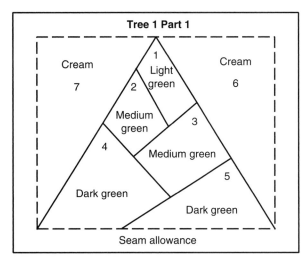

Cream 7

1 Light green

2

Medium green

3

4

Medium green

Dark green

5

Dark green

Seam allowance

Cream 6

Tree 2 Part 1

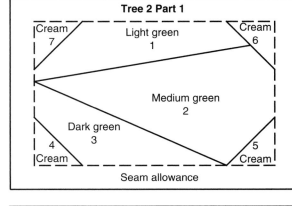

Cream 7

Light green 1

Cream 6

Medium green 2

Dark green 3

4 Cream

5 Cream

Seam allowance

Tree 1 Part 2

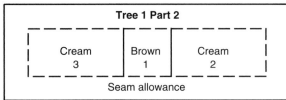

Cream 3 | Brown 1 | Cream 2

Seam allowance

Tree 2 Part 2

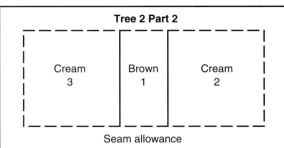

Cream 3 | Brown 1 | Cream 2

Seam allowance

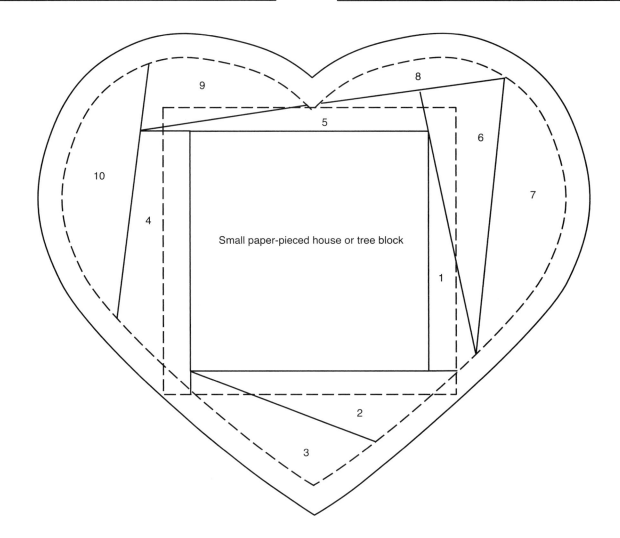

Small paper-pieced house or tree block

9

8

5

6

10

4

7

1

2

3

In the Cabin BY SUE HARVEY

Try paper piecing these Log Cabin coasters. Each coaster has a different design.

PROJECT SPECIFICATIONS

Coaster Size: 4¼" x 4¼"
Block Size: 4¼" x 4¼"
Number of Blocks: 4

MATERIALS FOR THE SET

- Fat quarter green print for strips and backing
- 10" x 10" square cream print
- 5" x 5" square burgundy print
- 10" x 10" square batting
- Dark green all-purpose thread
- Basic sewing supplies and tools and tracing paper

CUTTING FOR THE SET

1. Cut four squares each green print and batting 4¾" x 4¾".

2. Cut several strips green and cream fabrics 1" by fabric width.

3. Cut four squares burgundy print 1¾" x 1¾" for centers.

INSTRUCTIONS

1. Follow instructions for Paper-Pieced Blocks on page 2 to complete the set. ■

Pineapple Log Cabin Coaster
Placement Diagram
4¹/₄" x 4¹/₄"

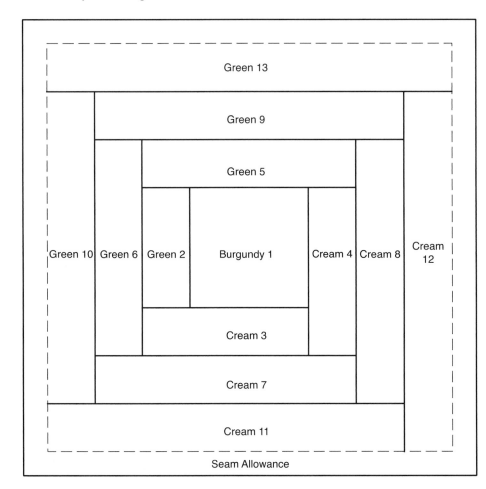

Green 25 · Cream 18 · Green 22

Cream 10 · Green 14

Green 17 · Green 9 · Cream 2 · Green 6

Cream 21 · Cream 13 · Cream 5 · Burgundy 1 · Cream 3 · Cream 11 · Cream 19

Green 8 · Cream 4 · Green 7

Green 16 · Green 15

Cream 12

Green 24 · Cream 20 · Green 23

Seam Allowance

**Pineapple Full-Size
Paper-Piecing Pattern**

Green 13

Green 9

Green 5

Green 10 · Green 6 · Green 2 · Burgundy 1 · Cream 4 · Cream 8 · Cream 12

Cream 3

Cream 7

Cream 11

Seam Allowance

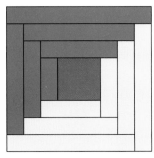

Log Cabin Coaster
Placement Diagram
4¹/₄" x 4¹/₄"

**Log Cabin Full-Size
Paper-Piecing Pattern**

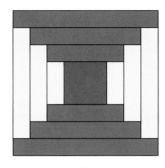

Courthouse Steps Coaster
Placement Diagram
$4\frac{1}{4}$" x $4\frac{1}{4}$"

**Courthouse Steps Full-Size
Paper-Piecing Pattern**

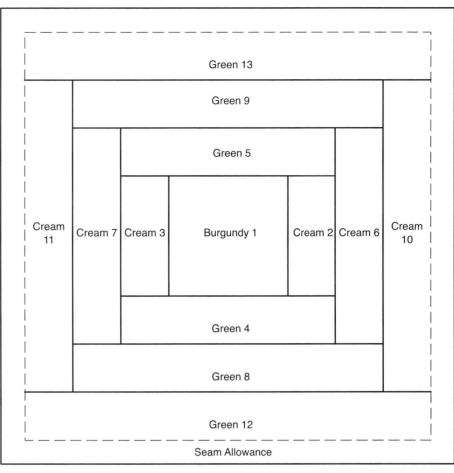

Green 13

Green 9

Green 5

Cream 11 | Cream 7 | Cream 3 | Burgundy 1 | Cream 2 | Cream 6 | Cream 10

Green 4

Green 8

Green 12

Seam Allowance

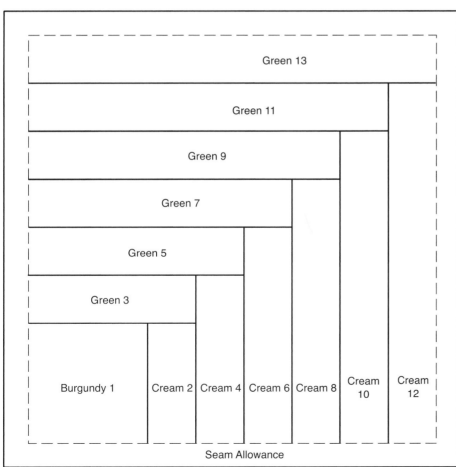

Green 13

Green 11

Green 9

Green 7

Green 5

Green 3

Burgundy 1 | Cream 2 | Cream 4 | Cream 6 | Cream 8 | Cream 10 | Cream 12

Seam Allowance

**Half Log Cabin Full-Size
Paper-Piecing Pattern**

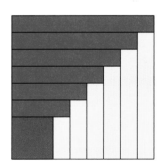

Half Log Cabin Coaster
Placement Diagram
$4\frac{1}{4}$" x $4\frac{1}{4}$"

Autumn Leaves

BY JOYCE LIVINGSTON

There are dozens of autumn leaves hiding in your scrap bag ready to share with family and friends.

PROJECT SPECIFICATIONS
Coaster Size: Size varies

MATERIALS
- An assortment of print scraps each at least 8" x 8" square—2 for each finished leaf
- Scrap pieces of batting 8" x 8" square
- Contrasting all-purpose thread
- Basic sewing supplies and tools, and small sharp scissors

INSTRUCTIONS
1. Prepare template for leaf shape using one of the patterns given or a leaf from your favorite tree. Mark vein lines.

2. Trace shape on the right side of one print square.

3. Place another print square right side down on a flat surface; lay a batting square on top. Place the traced square right side up on the batting; pin the three layers together.

4. Set the sewing machine to a medium-width zigzag stitch. Stitch on the marked lines on the top fabric piece, removing pins as you sew.

5. Stitch vein lines as marked on pattern, backstitching at beginning and end to lock stitches.

6. Using small sharp scissors, trim away excess fabric and batting as close to stitching as possible, being careful not to clip into stitching. **Note:** *If you slip and cut stitches, a touch of clear nail polish will hold them in place or you may re-stitch over that area.* ■

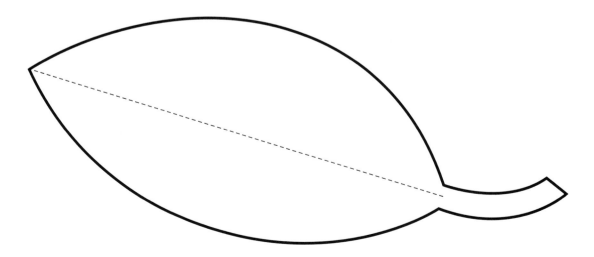

Triangles & Squares

BY RUTH M. SWASEY

Simple squares and triangles combine to make easy-to-piece designs to brighten any table.

PROJECT SPECIFICATIONS

Coaster Size: 5" x 5"
Block Size: 4½" x 4½"
Number of Blocks: 4

MATERIALS FOR THE SET

- Fat quarter each white, blue and green prints
- 12" x 12" square backing fabric
- 12" x 12" square light-weight batting
- 2¾ yards self-made or purchased binding
- White all-purpose thread
- Basic sewing tools and supplies

INSTRUCTIONS

1. Cut four squares batting 5" x 5" and four squares backing fabric 5" x 5". Cut four 24" pieces prepared bias binding.

2. Prepare templates using pattern pieces given. Cut as directed for each coaster as indicated in separate cutting charts.

3. Join pieces to make units referring to unit piecing diagram given for each design. Join units to complete blocks referring to the block piecing diagram given for each block.

4. Finish coasters referring to Binding and Quilting instructions on pages 2 and 3. ∎

Bear Paw Track Template Cutting Chart

I—Cut 4 each white & blue prints

L—Cut 1 blue print & 2 each green & white prints

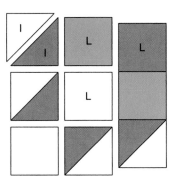

Bear Paw Track Units
Piece units as shown.

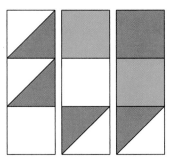

Bear Paw Track
Block Piecing Diagram
Lay out pieces to complete 1
Bear Paw Track block.

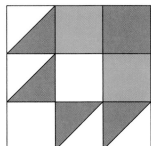

Bear Paw Track
Placement Diagram
5" x 5"

Diagonal Squares Template Cutting Chart

T—Cut 4 blue print

V—Cut 6 white print

AA—Cut 2 green print

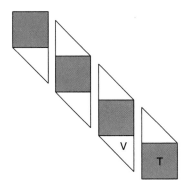

Diagonal Squares Units
Piece units as shown.

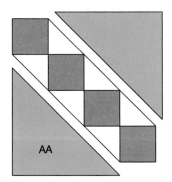

Diagonal Squares
Block Piecing Diagram
Lay out pieces to complete 1
Diagonal Squares block.

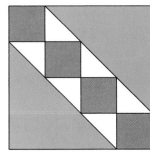

Diagonal Squares
Placement Diagram
5" x 5"

Four-Patch Triangles Template Cutting Chart

T—Cut 4 white print & 2 each blue and green prints

U—Cut 4 each blue & green prints

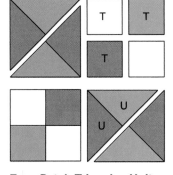

Four-Patch Triangles Units
Piece units as shown.

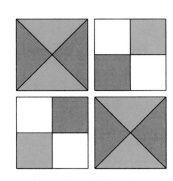

Four-Patch Triangles
Block Piecing Diagram
Lay out pieces to
complete 1 Four-Patch
Triangles block.

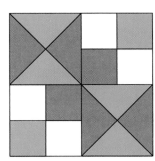

Four-Patch Triangles
Placement Diagram
5" x 5"

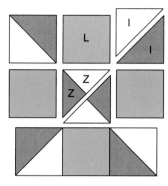

Tick-Tack Triangles Units
Piece units as shown.

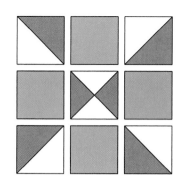

Tick-Tack Triangles
Block Piecing Diagram
Lay out pieces to
complete 1 Tick-Tack
Triangles block.

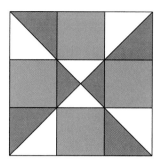

Tick-Tack Triangles
Placement Diagram
5" x 5"

Tick-Tack Triangles Template Cutting Chart

I—Cut 4 each white & blue prints

L—Cut 4 green print

Z—Cut 2 each white & blue prints

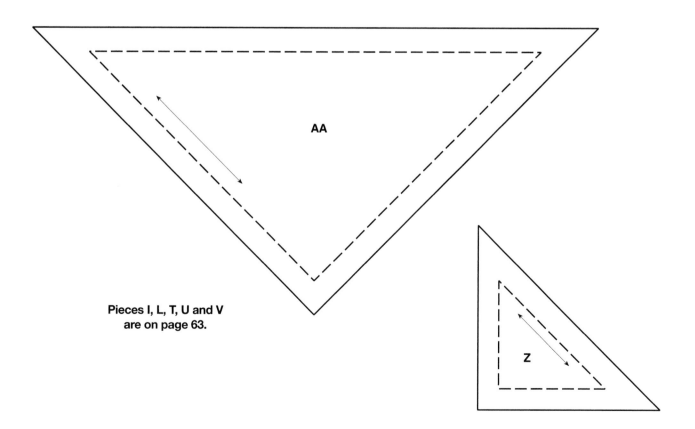

AA

**Pieces I, L, T, U and V
are on page 63.**

Z

Harvest Gold

BY RUTH M. SWASEY

Select a pretty print with leaf motifs to fit inside a circle for this perfect autumn set.

PROJECT SPECIFICATIONS

Coaster Size: 4½" diameter
Block Size: 4½" x 4½"
Number of Blocks: 4

MATERIALS FOR THE SET

- Fat quarter each leaf and gold prints
- 12" x 12" square backing fabric
- Gold all-purpose thread
- ¼ yard fusible web
- Basic sewing tools and supplies

INSTRUCTIONS

1. Cut four squares backing fabric 5" x 5".

2. Prepare QQ circle template from page 63 for design center. Choose a leaf-design motif from leaf print. Place template on leaf; cut out. Repeat for four leaf circles.

3. Prepare template for circle outline. Trace circle outline pattern on the paper side of the fusible web, leaving a margin between each shape and referring to the pattern for number to trace.

4. Cut out circle outline shapes, leaving a margin around each shape. Fuse circle outlines to the wrong side of the gold print. Cut out circle outlines on traced lines; remove paper backing.

5. Place a circle outline on the leaf circle; fuse in place referring to manufacturer's instructions.

6. Machine-appliqué shapes in place using a narrow zigzag stitch and gold all-purpose thread.

7. Cut backing pieces using appliquéd circle as a pattern.

HOUSE OF WHITE BIRCHES, BERNE, INDIANA 46711   WWW.WHITEBIRCHES.COM

8. Place appliquéd circle right sides together with backing fabric.

9. Stitch all around outer edges. Cut a small X on the backing fabric only. Turn right side out through X. Cut four 1" circles from fusible web; fuse to wrong side of gold print. Cut out fabric circles on traced lines; remove paper backing. Fuse over X cuts on backing to close opening to finish. ■

Autumn Leaves
Placement Diagram
4$\frac{1}{2}$" diameter

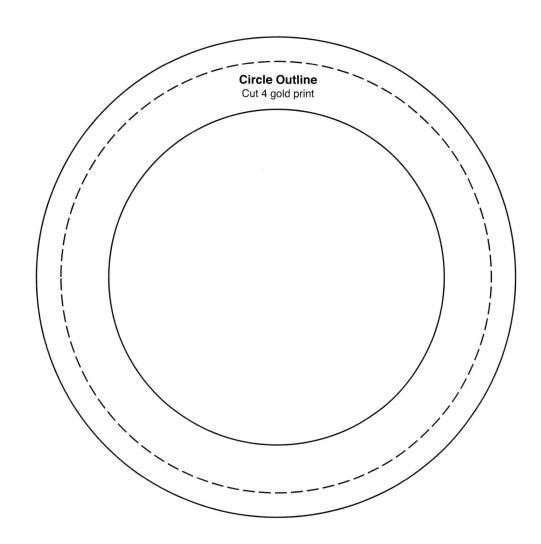

Circle Outline
Cut 4 gold print

Spring Coasters

BY SUE HARVEY

Celebrate the end of winter by making these coasters that feature spring motifs.

PROJECT SPECIFICATIONS

Coaster Size: 4½" x 4½"
Block Size: 4" x 4"
Number of Blocks: 4

MATERIALS FOR THE SET

- 10" x 10" square cream solid for background
- Scraps medium blue, light blue, yellow, green, light pink, dark pink, tan and light brown prints for appliqué
- Fat quarter floral print for backing and borders
- 10" x 10" square batting
- 10" x 10" square fusible web
- All-purpose thread to match appliqué fabrics
- All-purpose thread to match backing
- 6-strand pink embroidery floss
- Black, light blue and pink all-purpose thread
- Basic sewing supplies and tools

CUTTING FOR THE SET

1. Cut four squares cream solid 4½" x 4½" for background.

2. Cut four squares floral print 5" x 5" for backing.

3. Cut four squares batting 5" x 5".

4. Cut eight strips floral print ¾" x 4½" for borders.

5. Cut eight strips floral print ¾" x 5" for borders.

INSTRUCTIONS

Note: *Follow Special Instructions noted with individual patterns to complete this set.*

1. Sew ¾" x 4½" border strips to two opposite sides of the background fabric; press. Sew ¾" x 5" border strips to two remaining sides to form coaster; press.

2. Place coaster top right sides together with backing fabric; place a batting square under backing fabric.

3. Sew around edge using a ¼" seam allowance; leave a 2" opening on one side. Turn right side out; hand-stitch opening closed.

4. Bond fusible web to wrong side of fabric scraps to be used for appliqué following manufacturer's instructions.

5. Make a paper or plastic pattern for each piece to be appliquéd using pattern pieces given with pattern. Place patterns facedown on appropriate fabric scraps; trace and cut out each piece. Remove paper backing.

6. Place each piece on background fabric in the order indicated on the pattern pieces; fuse in place.

7. Satin-stitch around each shape using a coordinating thread in the top of the machine and thread to match the coaster backing in the bobbin.

Kite Special Instructions
1. Stitch kite crosspiece and string using black thread.

2. Stitch tail using pink thread.

3. Using 2 strands pink floss, go down through coaster top and back up through coaster; tie a small bow on the kite tail referring to the pattern. Repeat for the second bow.

Umbrella Special Instructions
1. Satin-stitch umbrella tip using black thread.

Bird's Nest Special Instructions
1. Cut inside of nest from wrong side of tan fabric; cut outside of nest from right side of fabric.

2. Cut out eggs as one large piece.

3. Stitch individual egg lines using light blue thread. ■

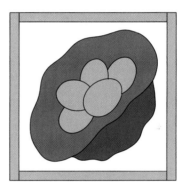

Bird s Nest Coaster
Placement Diagram
4¹/₂" x 4¹/₂"

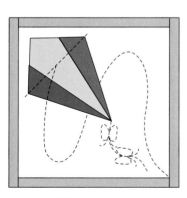

Kite Coaster
Placement Diagram
4¹/₂" x 4¹/₂"

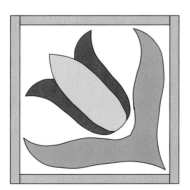

Tulip Coaster
Placement Diagram
4¹/₂" x 4¹/₂"

Umbrella Coaster
Placement Diagram
4¹/₂" x 4¹/₂"

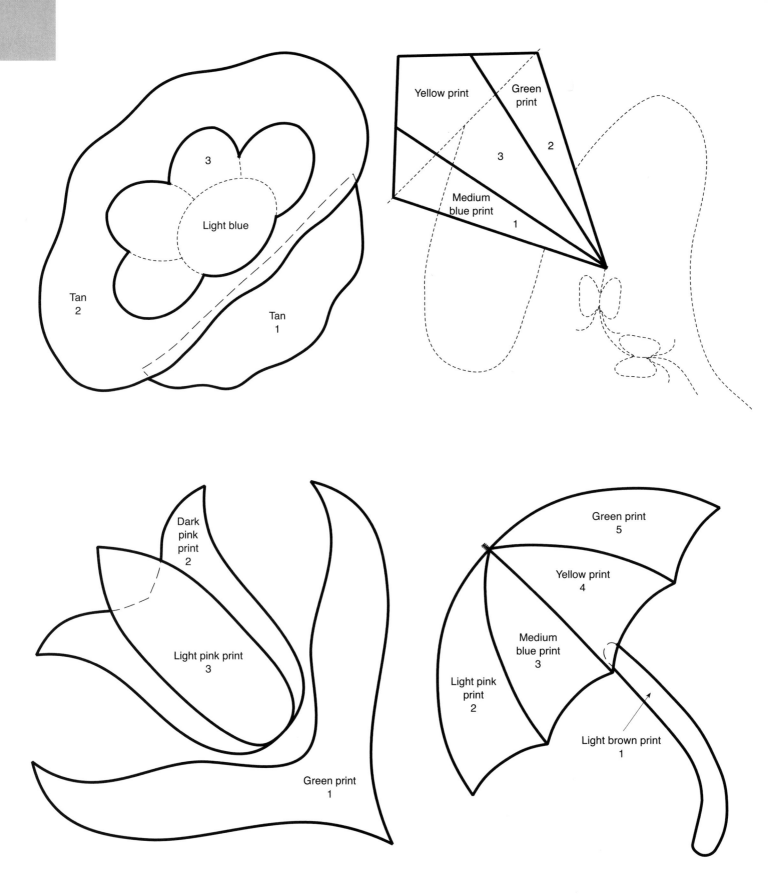

3

Light blue

Tan
2

Tan
1

Yellow print

Green
print

3

2

Medium
blue print

1

Dark
pink
print
2

Light pink print
3

Green print
1

Green print
5

Yellow print
4

Medium
blue print
3

Light pink
print
2

Light brown print
1

Appliqué Triangles

BY RUTH M. SWASEY

The coasters in this set have a triangular shape to frame the flowers inside.

PROJECT SPECIFICATIONS

Coaster Size: 7" x 7" x 7"
Block Size: 6¼" x 6¼" x 6¼"
Number of Blocks: 4

MATERIALS FOR THE SET

- Fat quarter each green, dark blue, light blue, rose and white prints
- 16" x 16" square backing fabric
- 16" x 16" square light-weight batting
- 2¾ yards self-made or purchased binding
- Rose all-purpose thread
- ½ yard fusible web
- Basic sewing tools and supplies

INSTRUCTIONS

1. Cut batting and backing pieces referring to the cutting charts. Cut four 24" pieces prepared bias binding.

2. Prepare templates using full-size designs given. Trace shapes onto paper side of fusible web. Cut out shapes, leaving a margin around each piece.

3. Fuse shapes to fabric referring to the cutting charts for color and number to cut. Cut out shapes on traced lines; remove paper backing.

4. Arrange shapes on 1A background piece in numerical order referring to the drawing for chosen design.

5. Fuse shapes in place referring to manufacturer's instructions.

6. Machine-appliqué shapes in place using a narrow zigzag stitch.

7. Finish coasters referring to Binding and Quilting instructions on pages 2 and 3. ∎

Ball Flower Template Cutting Chart

1A—Cut 1 white print, batting & backing
1E—Cut 3 green print
1G—Cut 1 light blue print
1F—Cut 1 dark blue print

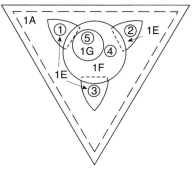

Ball Flower Appliqué Order
Arrange pieces on 1A in
numerical order as shown.

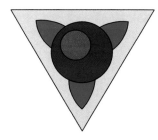

Ball Flower
Placement Diagram
7" x 7" x 7"

Petal Flower Template Cutting Chart

1A—Cut 1 white print, batting & backing
1G—Cut 1 dark blue print
1L—Cut 2 rose print
1M—Cut 1 light blue print
1N—Cut 2 green print

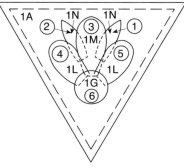

Petal Flower Appliqué Order
Arrange pieces on 1A in
numerical order as shown.

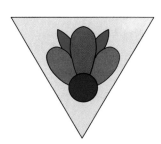

Petal Flower
Placement Diagram
7" x 7" x 7"

Tulip Triangle Template Cutting Chart

1A—Cut 1 each white print, batting & backing
1B—Cut 2 green print
1C—Cut 1 rose print
1D—Cut 1 dark blue print

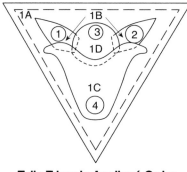

Tulip Triangle Appliqué Order
Arrange pieces on 1A in
numerical order as shown.

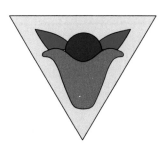

Tulip Triangle
Placement Diagram
7" x 7" x 7"

Square Flower Template Cutting Chart

1A—Cut 1 white print, batting & backing
1H—Cut 3 green print
1I—Cut 1 rose print
1J—Cut 1 dark blue print
1K—Cut 1 light blue print

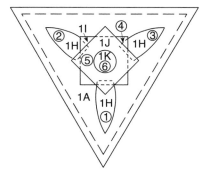

Square Flower Appliqué Order
Arrange pieces on 1A in
numerical order as shown.

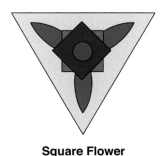

Square Flower
Placement Diagram
7" x 7" x 7"

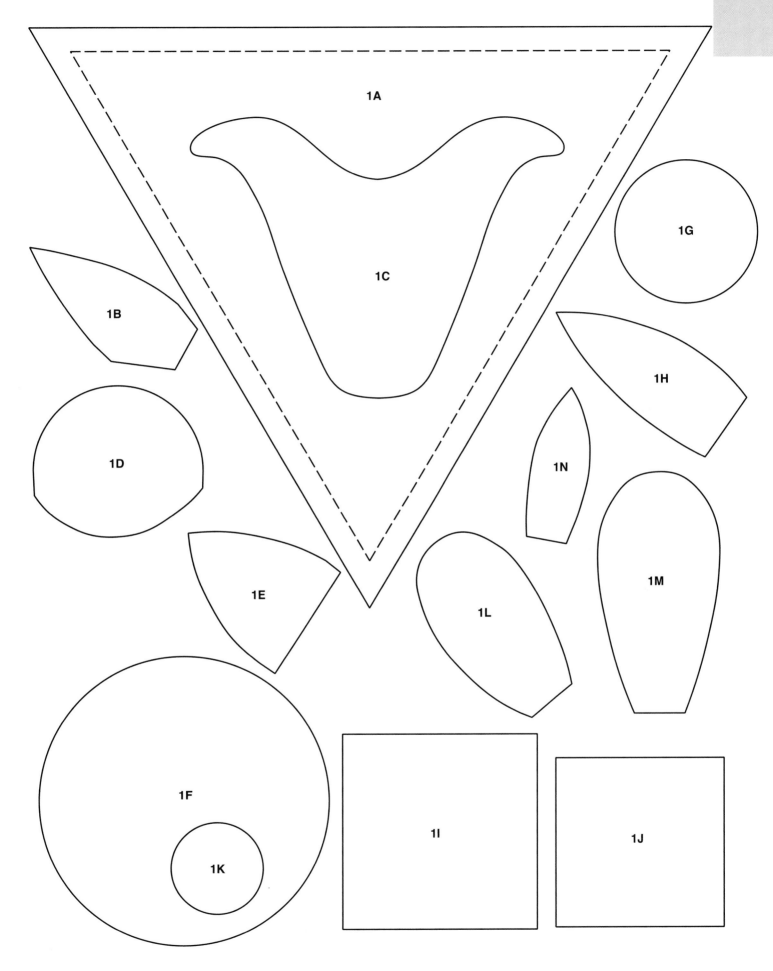

1A

1C

1G

1B

1H

1D

1N

1E

1M

1L

1F

1K

1I

1J

Happy Easter

BY JANICE LOEWENTHAL

Pastel fabric scraps and small squares of batting are all you need to make these neat coasters with Easter-design motifs.

PROJECT SPECIFICATIONS
Coaster Size: 4½" x 4½"
Block Size: 4" x 4"
Number of Blocks: 4

MATERIALS FOR THE SET
- Fat quarter light blue print for background
- Fat quarter pink print for binding
- Scraps assorted prints for appliqué
- ⅛ yard pre-quilted muslin
- All-purpose thread to match or contrast with fabrics
- ⅛ yard fusible web
- ⅛ yard tear-off fabric stabilizer
- Black and white permanent fabric pens
- Basic sewing supplies and tools

INSTRUCTIONS
1. Chose one appliqué motif. Prepare templates for each shape using full-size pattern given.

2. Trace shapes onto paper side of fusible web referring to pattern for number to cut. Cut out shapes leaving a margin beyond traced lines.

3. Fuse shapes to fabric scraps using colors as desired. Cut out shapes on traced lines; remove paper backing.

4. Cut one square light blue print 4½" x 4½". Center motif on square referring to full-size pattern and Placement Diagram for positioning of pieces; fuse in place.

5. Cut a square of fabric stabilizer 4½" x 4½". Using threads to contrast or match fabrics, machine-appliqué around each shape. Remove stabilizer when stitching is complete.

Bunny
Placement Diagram
4¹/₂" x 4¹/₂"

Easter Basket
Placement Diagram
4¹/₂" x 4¹/₂"

Eggs
Placement Diagram
4¹/₂" x 4¹/₂"

Little Chick
Placement Diagram
4¹/₂" x 4¹/₂"

6. Cut one square pre-quilted muslin 4½" x 4½"; pin behind fused motif. Place the appliquéd square on top of the muslin square wrong sides together; pin to hold.

7. Complete following Binding and Quilting instructions on pages 2 and 3. *Note: For Little Chick design, use black and white permanent fabric pens to make eyes, referring to pattern for placement.* ■

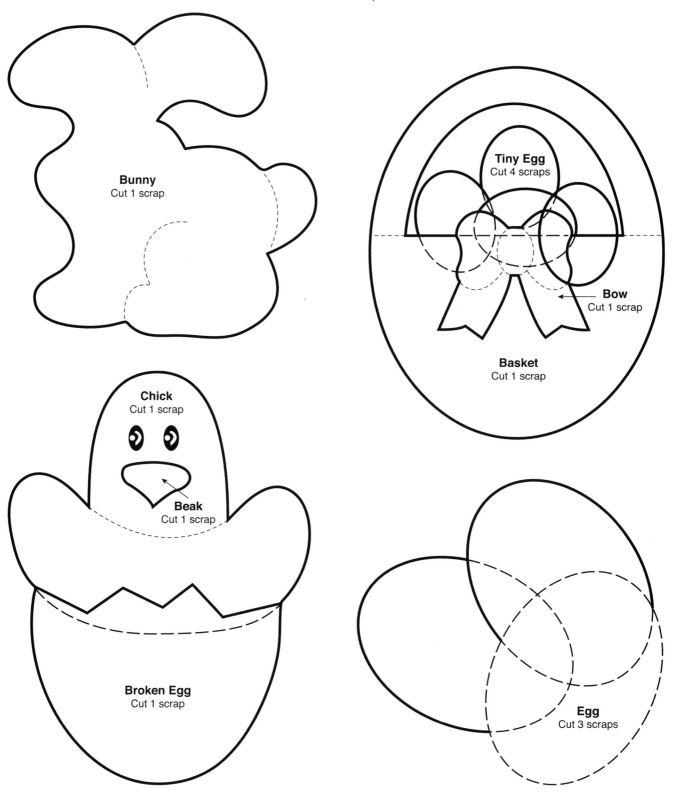

Autumn Frolic

BY SUE HARVEY

As the harvest season is in full swing and the leaves begin to change and fall, make this coaster set to include the colors of the season.

PROJECT SPECIFICATIONS
Coaster Size: 4½" x 4½"
Block Size: 4" x 4"
Number of Blocks: 4

MATERIALS FOR THE SET
- 10" x 10" square cream solid for background
- Scraps brown/gold, autumn multicolor, light yellow/green, dark yellow/green, olive, green, red, orange and brown prints for appliqué
- Fat quarter fall leaf print for backing and borders
- 10" x 10" square batting
- 10" x 10" square fusible web
- All-purpose thread to match appliqué fabrics and backing
- Dark green and dark brown all-purpose thread
- Basic sewing supplies and tools

CUTTING FOR THE SET
1. Cut four squares cream solid 4½" x 4½" for background.

2. Cut four squares fall leaf print 5" x 5" for backing.

3. Cut four squares batting 5" x 5".

4. Cut eight strips fall leaf print ¾" x 4½" for borders.

5. Cut eight strips fall leaf print ¾" x 5" for borders.

INSTRUCTIONS
Note: *Follow Special Instructions noted with individual patterns to complete this set.*

1. Sew ¾" x 4½" border strips to two opposite sides of the background fabric; press. Sew ¾" x 5" border strips to two remaining sides to form coaster; press.

2. Place coaster top right sides together with backing fabric; place a batting square under backing fabric.

3. Sew around edge using a ¼" seam allowance; leave a 2" opening on one side. Turn right side out; hand-stitch opening closed.

4. Bond fusible web to wrong side of fabric scraps to be used for appliqué following manufacturer's instructions.

5. Make a paper or plastic pattern for each piece to be appliquéd using pattern pieces given. Place patterns facedown on appropriate fabric scraps; trace and cut out each piece. Remove paper backing.

6. Place each piece on background fabric in the order indicated on the pattern pieces; fuse in place.

7. Satin-stitch around each shape using a coordinating thread in the top of the machine and thread to match the coaster backing in the bobbin.

Apple Special Instructions
1. Stitch stem base line using dark brown thread.

Maple Leaf Special Instructions
1. Stitch leaf veins using dark brown thread.

Pumpkin Special Instructions
1. Stitch tendrils and leaf veins using dark green thread.

2. Stitch pumpkin lines using dark brown thread. ▪

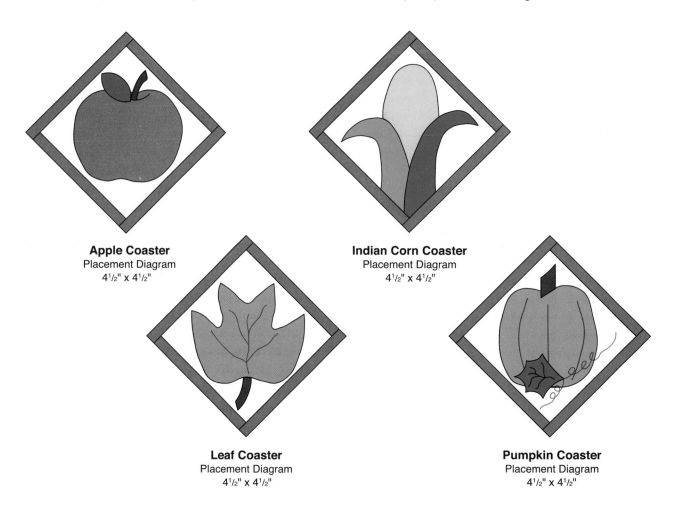

Apple Coaster
Placement Diagram
4¹/₂" x 4¹/₂"

Indian Corn Coaster
Placement Diagram
4¹/₂" x 4¹/₂"

Leaf Coaster
Placement Diagram
4¹/₂" x 4¹/₂"

Pumpkin Coaster
Placement Diagram
4¹/₂" x 4¹/₂"

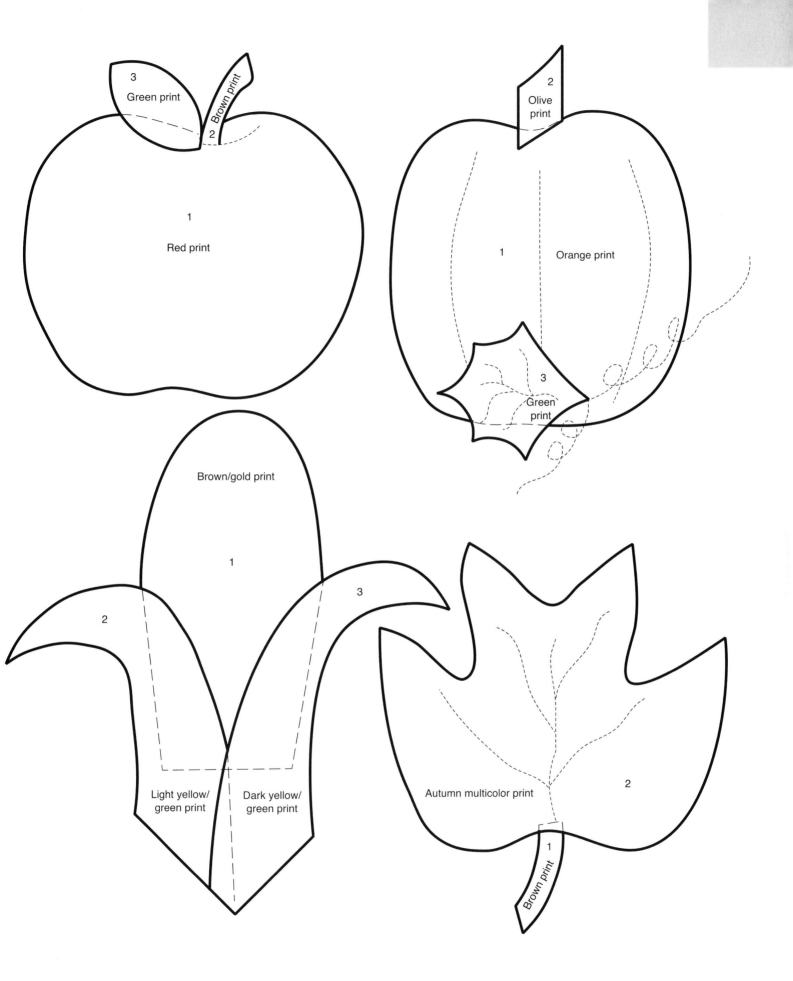

3

Green print

Brown print

2

1

Red print

2

Olive print

1

Orange print

3

Green print

Brown/gold print

1

2

3

Light yellow/
green print

Dark yellow/
green print

Autumn multicolor print

2

1

Brown print

Winter Fun

BY SUE HARVEY

Use these coasters under mugs of cocoa to warm up after playing outside on a cold winter day.

PROJECT SPECIFICATIONS
Coaster Size: 4½" x 4½"
Block Size: 4" x 4"
Number of Blocks: 4

MATERIALS FOR THE SET
- 10" x 10" square cream solid for background
- Scraps red/black check, red dot, tan, dark brown, gray and blue prints and white solid for appliqué
- Scraps red and white felt for appliqué
- Fat quarter dark blue/light blue print for backing and borders
- 10" x 10" square batting
- 10" x 10" square fusible web
- All-purpose thread to match appliqué fabrics
- Blue all-purpose thread to match backing
- Black and brown all-purpose thread
- Permanent blue fabric pen
- Basic sewing supplies and tools

CUTTING FOR THE SET
1. Cut four squares cream solid 4½" x 4½" for background.

2. Cut four squares dark blue/light blue print 5" x 5" for backing.

3. Cut four squares batting 5" x 5".

4. Cut eight strips dark blue/light blue print ¾" x 4½" for borders.

5. Cut eight strips dark blue/light blue print ¾" x 5" for borders.

INSTRUCTIONS
Note: *Follow Special Instructions noted with individual patterns to complete this set.*

1. Sew ¾" x 4½" border strips to two opposite sides of the background fabric; press. Sew ¾" x 5" border strips to two remaining sides to form coaster top; press.

2. Place coaster top right sides together with backing fabric; place a batting square under backing fabric.

3. Sew around edge using a ¼" seam allowance; leave a 2" opening on one side. Turn right side out; hand-stitch opening closed.

4. Bond fusible web to wrong side of fabric scraps to be used for appliqué following manufacturer's instructions.

5. Make a paper or plastic pattern for each piece to be appliquéd using pattern pieces given with pattern. Place patterns facedown on appropriate fabric scraps; trace and cut out each piece. Remove paper backing.

6. Place each piece on background fabric in the order indicated on the pattern pieces; fuse in place.

7. Satin-stitch around each shape using a

coordinating thread in the top of the machine and thread to match the coaster backing in the bobbin.

Snowman Special Instructions
1. Stitch mouth and eyes using black thread.

2. Stitch twig arms using brown thread.

Skates Special Instructions
1. Stitch skate laces using black thread.

Sled Special Instructions
1. Write the letters on sled using permanent blue fabric pen.

Hat & Mittens Special Instructions
1. Fussy cut blue fabric with stars for mittens. ■

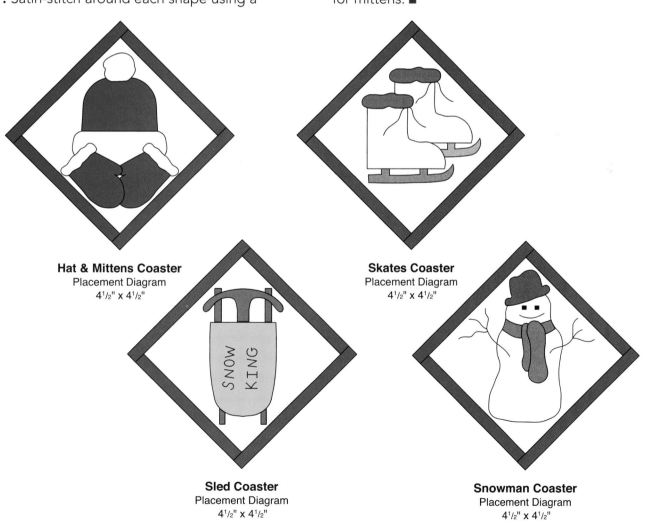

Hat & Mittens Coaster
Placement Diagram
4¹/₂" x 4¹/₂"

Skates Coaster
Placement Diagram
4¹/₂" x 4¹/₂"

Sled Coaster
Placement Diagram
4¹/₂" x 4¹/₂"

Snowman Coaster
Placement Diagram
4¹/₂" x 4¹/₂"

Dark brown
5

2

3

Red/black
check
4

White felt
1

Red felt

5

6

White 2

White
4

1
Gray print 1

Gray print 3

Red dot

Red dot
5

2

1

Sled

SNOW KING

Tan print
6

3

4

Red dot

White felt
7

Hat & Mittens

Blue print
1

White felt
2

White felt 5

White felt 6

Blue print
4

Blue print
3

Common Templates

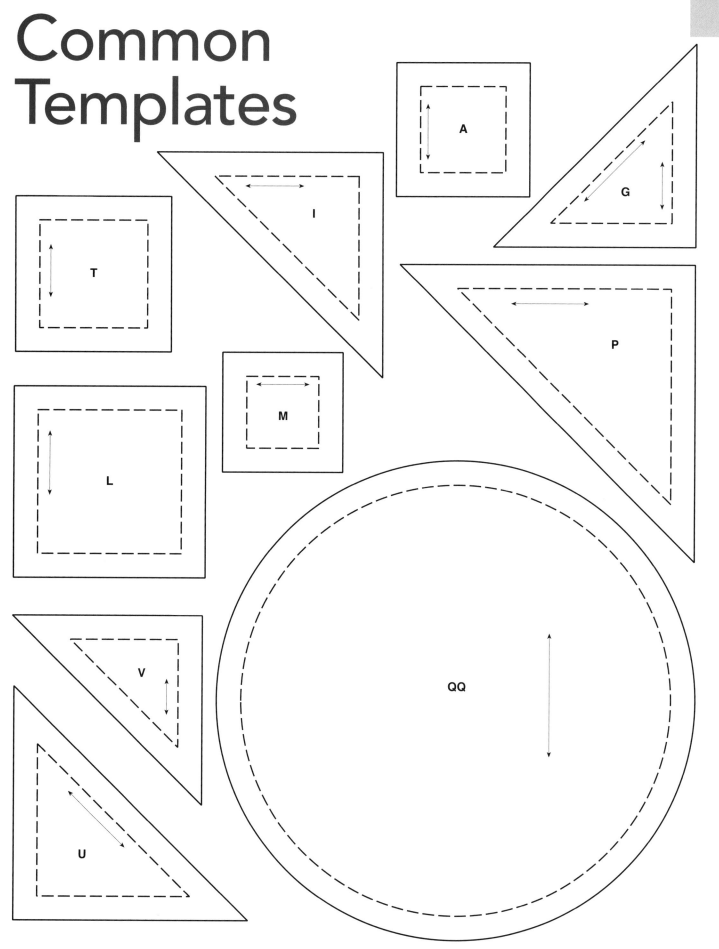

A

G

I

T

P

M

L

QQ

V

U

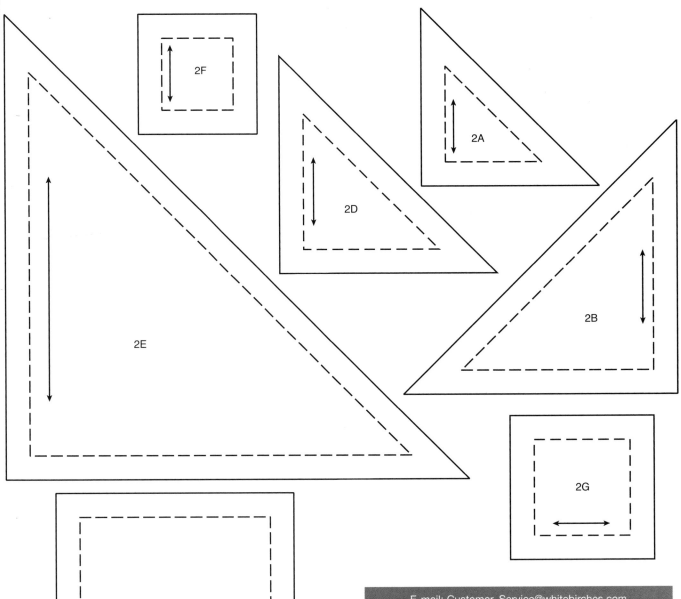

2F

2A

2D

2E

2B

2G

2H

2I

HOUSE of WHITE BIRCHES
PUBLISHERS SINCE 1947

E-mail: Customer_Service@whitebirches.com

Quick-to-Quilt Coasters is published by House of White Birches, 306 East Parr Road, Berne, IN 46711, telephone (260) 589-4000. Printed in USA. Copyright © 2005 House of White Birches.

RETAIL STORES: If you would like to carry this pattern book or any other House of White Birches publications, call the Wholesale Department at Annie's Attic to set up a direct account: (903) 636-4303. Also, request a complete listing of publications available from House of White Birches.

Every effort has been made to ensure that the instructions in this pattern book are complete and accurate. We cannot, however, take responsibility for human error, typographical mistakes or variations in individual work.

ISBN: 1-59217-098-6
2 3 4 5 6 7 8 9

STAFF
Editors: Jeanne Stauffer, Sandra L. Hatch
Associate Editor: Dianne Schmidt
Technical Artist: Connie Rand
Copy Supervisor: Michelle Beck
Copy Editors: Nicki Lehman,
    Mary O'Donnell
Graphic Arts Supervisor: Ronda Bechinski

Graphic Artists: Debby Keel,
    Edith Teegarden
Art Director: Brad Snow
Assistant Art Director: Nick Pierce
Photography: Tammy Christian, Christena
    Green, Don Clark, Matthew Owen
Photo Stylists: Tammy Nussbaum,
    Tammy M. Smith